No Privacy
"My Life's An Open Book"

$yourfavoritecatfish

yourfavoritecatfish

your_favorite_catfish

elnewman52@gmail.com

(989) 403-0692

amazon

Author Ericka
Newman

PRIVACY

By Ericka Newman

www.Soarbookpublishing@yahoo.com
www.soarbookpublishing.com

ISBN 9781076776228

Allow God to Reveal
You to You!

Acknowledgments

When I first started writing this, I told myself as well as others it was tons of people I would mention and thank. But I want to keep this simple.

First and foremost, I want to thank God, because with him all things are possible, you put God first and you'll never be last. I want to thank my parents Carl and April. I want to thank them for not just being my parents, but for the love support and discipline. For instilling the lifelong lessons that I'll have forever, I am who I am because of them.

My second set of parents Banesha and Dave, I thank them for not treating me like just Quas babymomma, but a part of their family, for welcoming me with open and loving arms.

My sister Latrice, for being "Momma number two. For being not just my sister but my friend. To all the rants she's had to listen to and all her problem I had to help her advice.

My siblings Carl, Robert, Danielle, Jarod, Karla, Sabrina and Shaquitta. My second set Ladaizja, Davion, Detavion, Tanaja, DaeDae, Quin, Jadaiya, NeAsia lil Dave and Rondarius,.My nieces and nephews, LaBriea, JaSyiah, D'Amari Anyilah, Sophia,Serenity, Nekhi and CJ. My biggest blessing, The girls who stole my heart, my reason for change and personal growth, my motivation my first true loves and they calls me mom, my Payton Armani and Kennedi Royale.

To Nikki, Shelley, Jim, Latretha, George, Marilyn, Nay Nay, KY, Armand, Toot, Taronda, Tre, John,and Kiana

To my uncles, Andre, Twon, Terry, James, and Troy, my aunt Angela and May. My godmom Demeka, my Bigmomma and grandma and granddad Cookie and Willie

To the amazing men that I've ever had the pleasure of meeting Devon Travers, Broderick Owens, Edward, Dametrus Cotton and Wesley Ramsey.

To all of my friends, the real MVP's Emoni, Erica, Demetra, Jameisha, Shatavia, Shontorria, Tiera ,Precious, Ashia and to the friends that I've had the pleasure of meeting MaRae, Jarquis, Marcadies, Ciara, BabySis, Keezy, Sei my brothers Dion Dugga Alantae Joe and Lontae

Mrs. Beluch and Mrs. Antra

To those who past away, You all will never be forgotten, Qua Southward, Brian Kelly, Ronnie Clemmons, Deleon Taylor, Maurice Burnett, Daruis Johnson, James Smothers my Big Momma Willie Tolden and Scott Most.

And last but not least, those who made this book possible, those who inspired every word, who were the reason for every emotion, every heartbreak, heartache and lessons I'll never forget. I wish I coulda named you all personally, but I don't need no lawsuits for defamation or slander.

Fall in *Love* with who God's *Calling* you to be.

Table of Contents

YOUR life IS WORTH LIVING

Privacy

Glen Greenwald says "There's nothing wrong with singing and dancing, yet you do it in private because you don't want to do it in front of others. You may not have nothing incriminating to hide but that doesn't mean you should be allowed to sing and dance in private. The world is split into good people and bad people but at the end of the day we are all just people, and we do things that we don't want to be seen. If you aren't doing anything wrong you don't have anything to hide or privacy doesn't matter, but yet take all kinds of steps to safe guard our privacy. Putting passwords on emails and social media, putting locks on bedroom and bathroom doors. All steps designed to prevent others from entering.

It's very hard when trying to explain privacy, it's a very shady area. Growing up as children, there was no such thing as privacy... I remember hearing my parents saying NO LOCKED DOORS!! I remembered I couldn't wait to get older so I wouldn't have to have my parents watching and monitoring my social media, always wanting to know where I was and who I was with. to be able to not even lock the door but just close it so I could escape from everybody without them thinking I was plotting and planning.

In school we are taught about all these laws regarding privacy, and are someone told that we are entitled to it.

1st amendment- protects the privacy of beliefs

3rd amendment- protects the privacy of home

4th amendment protects privacy against unreasonable searchers

5th amendment- protects self-incrimination which in turns protects privacy of personal information

9th amendment- protects privacy in ways was not specifically provided in the first 8 amendments

The older I've gotten and this is just me personally, privacy is still very confusing. If there's something about me that I don't want you to know, I won't disclose it. You will only know what I allow you to know. I hate when I see people who post everything about them on social media and then get mad when people go back talking about them. Like bruh chill, if you aint want us to know you shouldn't or wouldn't be posting it. That's like when I found out I was pregnant the second time, for a while, I felt like it wasn't anyone's business, I kept it to myself, because it was my personal life. And when I was ready to receive the backlash, the congratulations and all the other responses that came with it, I shared it. Mind you I'm grown and I could have just told friends and family, but hell word of mouth spreads like wildfire so I rather you hear it from the horse's mouth.

You wouldn't walk around ass naked if you knew you lived in a glass house? You wouldn't get freaky and do the nasty things with ya boyfriend if you knew your kids, parents, roommates or anybody else was watching or could hear you. If you knew people were watching you, or listening to you (recording you and could later use your own words against you to hurt or incriminate you) I bet you'd be more cautious of what you said and the things you do. It's like having everything you do being visible and make accessible to the public. I wouldn't get freaky and have no Kim and Ray j no Mimi and Niko moment if I knew it would get out. There are things that I swore to my family, friends, myself and God, that I would never do let alone have someone do those things to me. If my privacy was invaded it would make me seem like a liar. I would never admit, to letting a guy stick his thumb in my butt during sex even though the rapper Future made it seem like it was just a new trend now a days. I would not suck and lick his balls, lick and rub his toes none of that, I'd probably swear on the bible that unless someone saw me do it that they were a fucking liar.

Privacy isn't about having anything to hide, privacy is strictly having the option, or right to do things without having to do them in front of others, the right to do things behind closed doors without the eyes ears or judgement of other.

Throughout this novel you will really get to know me, the real me. You'll read my pain, my heart break, shame, and guilt. You'll know the most intimate details that only God himself knows about me. You're getting real life, raw emotions; know the story behind the face. Go ahead and judge if you want to, Hell they did it t Jesus so I know I aint got no sympathy or compassion coming my way.

You'll hear me talk about privacy a lot and I say this several times throughout this novel. I HAVE NO PRIVACY!! The moment I went through with the publication process my life became an open book, no pun intended. Literally you can go back to pages reread everything about me. I used to always say people only know what I allow them to know and to a certain degree that's still true. Although I might be breaking so many unwritten rules, street codes and etc. But at this point in my life, I don't even give a fuck. This is about me!! Me and only me, my life, the choices I've made and consequences of my actions. I'm too old for people's approvals anymore.

Just know that I'm giving you me, as much of myself as I've ever given anyone. Thinking about this I feel so vulnerable. I feel so out of pocket. But yet I feel my strongest. That after all these years I am able to tell my story. Able to tell you about the little bitch from small ass Saginaw, who grew up in the suburbs of Jersey born in Philadelphia.

Like Kevin Hart, you can laugh at my pain, laugh all the fuck you want.

As a mother I can't even eat, sleep or piss in peace. If I close any door. All I hear is "Mom what you doing??" "Open the door" "can I come in" I see feet at the door waiting for me to open it with smiling and mischievous faces.

And lastly, growing up parents instill in their children that until they become adults and start paying bills of their own, they have no privacy. And growing up I couldn't wait to be grown so people could stay the hell out of my business, but yet that was like the biggest lie of all, because although I'm an adult every time I turn around someone has their nose in my damn business. People questioning my past, present, and my future, parenting skills, my love life, and friendships, EVERYTHING I felt was nobody else's business was the local topic of conversation. My life, my privacy and I shouldn't have to explain myself to nobody.

I should have the right to do what I want without any critics, but also I learned in life that nothing we do in life is private. We are constantly being viewed, watched and talked about, by our peers, hell even strangers. If you don't want others to see or know anything you do. No Offense in my opinion you might as well be dead. Because as long as your living with a single breath in your body, you will be watched and judged. You will be judged and sometimes by those who don't have a leg to stand on, or a pot to piss in or window to throw it out of.

So again, I named it No Privacy, because to me I feel as if in no point in life we have no privacy. Nothing we do is personal anymore. So I couldn't think of a better title, than to call it something that everyone wants, but nobody really has. We invade others, but will beat a bitch bloody if they invade ours. Hypocritical? We demand it, we can't wait to have it but little do we know we never fully get it.

So I give you me, all of me, and I rather have someone who looking at my life, through my eyes, through my point of view, through my pain, my fears tears and emotions. You don't know my struggle. So I always try to remain humble and never think of myself any higher than anyone else, because you don't know what type of demons someone else may be battling.

I try my best to mind my own business and yes at times I fall short, and stick my nose where it doesn't belong. I find myself gossiping from time to time, watching and observing passing judgement on other. I'm only human, I fall short. I'm just here to let ya'll know I'm just like yall. I'm just an everyday person, I'm just Ericka, the daughter of April and Carl, the sister of Latrice and etc. The granddaughter of Cookie and Willie, the friends of Stasha, Meech, Meisha, Emoni and Erica, and the mother of Qua and Marcus child. I'm just a plain Jane with a story to tell, and by all means am I gonna tell it.

One of the hardest things in life to overcome are the situations that are happening to us currently. We stress, worry and contemplate how the hell we are going to get out of the predicament we are in. We are in every type of negative thinking possible. We feel people are against us, trying to see us fail and don't care about us at all. And I'm one of those people who think the worst of everybody and everybody. Nobody has to tell me that I'm my own worst enemy, toughest critic, all that. I expect so much of myself because, I know what I am capable of. Or when I have no control over what's going on, I break down, I cry and isolate myself. Because I have no one in my corner to help me, I'm always the one helping others but who do I call on when I need saving?

It's hard to talk about something you're currently going through, because you fear judgement from others, on how you should or could have been handling the situation. It was hard writing these stories because as I wrote these words I relived the experiences, but it was a little easeful to know that they were situations that already happened, that I survived from and are over and done with. I was able to sit back and laugh at myself and say "Girl you a big as dummy" but at the end of it all I was so glad those events were over. Because when they were happening to me, I thought I was going to die thought I wasn't going to overcome and let go of these people. I learned that God will give you all the signs that people aren't right for you and to let them go. Hell he will even show you them at their worst let you see their true colors but until you are truly and fully ready to remove them and let them go you are going to continue to suffer. I think God must have thought I was dumb and liked hurting because I kept putting myself in situations where I gave someone the power to control me, to hurt me, use me and I lost myself. Never let someone have that much power and control over you, where you have no say so or no voice about your own life. Nobody is going to do for you the way you do for yourself.

I thank the Lord everyday, for bringing me out of the darkest times of my life. I sit back and think "If it had not been for the Lord on my side, tell me where would I be, where would I be?"

As you read these chapters and stories, I want you to remember these are actual events, these are things I went through, and not only did I go through them; I want you to know that I overcame them. I am able to sit here today and share my story with you. You will go through my journey as I have already gone through it. And you may find that my story may not be so different from yours.

Think about a time when you knew you were getting played, and were too dumb to care or too stupid to see. Think of those relationships that were toxic and no good. Those relationships your friends and family told you to get out of. Think of the days when you thought your world was going to end if you weren't with the person. These are those kind of stories. Stories that make you think of what you been through, dealt with and most of all overcome. These are those type of stories that are heartfelt, you feel every word, because you can relate. And that's all I'm trying to accomplish. I'm an everyday person, going through everyday problems. I want to be relatable to people. And what better way to relate to ya'll than to share my story.

Privacy isn't about secretivty, it's a matter of having the options to let others in.

Prologue

Ever been in love? Ever had your heart broke? Dealt with liars, cheaters, users, abusers, married men, players, men with more baby momma issues than you've seen on an episode of Maury? The men who couldn't stay out of jail even if you paid them? Ever had a guy who loved you? But you didn't know what it meant to love and give love in return cuz you were so used to dealing with fuck boys? You couldn't pinpoint a real man even with all the signs right in front of you? Or have you ever treated someone wrong and tried to justify it by saying hurt people hurt people? Or said that I thought he was cheating so I cheated too? Ever just jumped to conclusions without knowing all the facts?

Have You? Well if you have then your just like me and probably others out here exactly like us. These type of men have been out here since who knows, ya momma grandma, aunty even the women in your life who you think are the most strongest fearless, or heartless, people you know done came across dudes like this. Ever had someone try to warn you about a boy and they say "I know the type". Well when they say that, you really better listen and take that information and let it sink in. Now don't get me wrong, you will have those people who just don't like your significant other, and will do anything to stop it.

The only thing that makes you and me different are the names of our stories, how we handled and got through them, and who knows you story might be more emotional, more of a struggle. We all have stories to tell, I just so happen to be crazy enough, bold enough and brave enough to share mine. I wanted someone to know that, Yes I understand, I've been there, I might not know your story personally, but I know mine I know what I've done, what I've been through, what I've seen and most of all what I've overcome. And everything that I've been through has made who I am. I no longer am ashamed of my past, because I once heard every saint was a sinner, and every sinner has a past.

I wrote this book back in July of 2009 and I've been putting it off, and prolonging it, and telling myself I'll get to it later. But in the process of waiting to finish this novel all I did was give myself more stories to have the chance to experience with you all. Now don't get me wrong people come and go everyday and the stories never stop. But I think I picked the perfect point to stop waiting for stories to come along and tell the ones that I already have.

I wrote this book, honestly, for those who always have something to say about Ericka. Those who think they know more about me than I know about myself. For those who are always talking, well I'm gonna give you something to talk about. You think you know but you have no idea. I'm here only to educate and shut up a few people. I came to set the record straight to put facts to the rumors and accusations. You gone get it all straight from the horse's mouth. So if there's anything you think you know, anything you may heard you might get the answers you want after you read these stories.

Some of my characters, if you knew the true identity, you'd realize these people are everyday people, ordinary people. People you know, these people are peoples sons, might be your brother, a boy you grew up with and knew all your life, might be ya boyfriend, might be your baby's father. But once again the purpose of me telling all this doesn't chance. I'm someone's daughter, I'm someone's mother. I might be a girl you grew up with and you'd never imagine that someone would even do those things to me. You might be my best friend and not even know some of the things I've been through, cuz it's just too much to wrap around ya brain.

For a while now, I've been holding back these words, these thoughts, these feelings. Afraid of what people were gonna say, gonna think, but I must admit the older I've gotten I've come to the realization that it doesn't matter what people think of me or say about me. All that matters is what I think of myself. I'm the only one who has to live this life. And people will talk regardless if good or bad. I don't have the time, nor the energy to waste worrying about people who really don't give a fuck about me.

I'm just blessed to say thank God, I don't look like what I've been through. Although there days when I feel shitty, weak, defeated, tired, and didn't know if I was going to make it to tomorrow, look at me now. Standing tall, ten toes down. Through all the shit that has gone on, I remember this too shall pass. And it has. It had been rough, but God gives his strongest battles to his toughest soldiers. One thing about life is that it waits for nobody.

You keep waiting and waiting hoping for change and different results, sorry to tell you, YOU ARE A FUCKING FOOL!! Become the change you want to see. If you don't like what you're seeing, then change it. The same way you would change an outfit that no longer looks or feels right. Change it, like the old hairstyle that's been up for too long. Give yourself a new look up, refresh yourself. Change it, like a shitty ass diaper that's stinking up the place and you're ready to get that shit off you. When you're tired of the bullshit and drama that's going on around you, eventually you'll realize that somethings gotta give. I once heard on the movie "Notorious" We can't change the world until we change ourselves.

And I must admit those have had to be the wisest words I've ever heard. But it took me a long time to let that marinate and sink into not only my mind, but my spirit. I had to not only think it, but live it. Those words became my thoughts and those thoughts became my actions. When they say actions speak louder, than words, you have to let those words be your foundation and build.

I'm at a point in my life where I really got my shit together. I mean I'm doing what I have to because it's what I'm supposed to be doing. As a woman as an adult and as a mother. Own apartment, car, stay with a job, even though anyone who knows me knows I will up in leave in a heartbeat, cuz I don't have time to deal with the fuckary. I worked so hard to get to where I'm at. I remember the struggle like it was yesterday. No car, in the middle of winter having to walk and stand outside with my neighbor waiting for the bus. Payton stayed sick, because I always had to bring her out into that cold air. Walking to work, rain, sleet, snow, hot as weather, or leaving my home at 4:30 in the morning. Asking my best friend Tay and DeeDee or Scott would we stay the night so they could watch Payton while I worked.

I remember crying because I felt like I was a bad mother, that I wasn't ready, but I also remember all that I sacrificed, to get to where I'm at today.

At one point in my life, I thought I had it all figured out. I was in a good space, a very good space actually. After several years of struggling, trying to figure out not just the facts of life, but trying to discover myself, who I am, who I was and who I am trying to become. I spent so much time, wasting my time, never fully understanding how valuable and precious my time was. Although 2017 had been a rough year, it was the year of "SELF" for me. And I say that because I spent so many of my years trying to please others, accommodate be considerate and compassionate towards others feelings, I forgot about my own. From being pregnant, a broken leg, being on crutches, to being on Catfish and everything in between. Pretty much if you name it I've dealt with it in 2017. Ended a two year relationship that year. Went from one of my best friends to my biggest enemy. I spent so much time being angry and mad at everyone but myself. I had to do a lot of "Self-Examination" I had to put on my big girl panties and stop fearing "self" intimidation. Yes, I'm my own biggest critic, but I'm also my biggest supporter. No one is going to do for me the way I do. Yes there were people who looked out, they were people who stood ten toes tall thru it all, and were by my side and I genuinely thank those people. Because I was going through a situation and they made sure that when I was at my lowest they reassured me that this too shall pass.

2017 was the year of self-love, self-hate, self-critism, self-worth, and self-esteem. It's funny you would have thought, I was meeting myself for the very first time. I couldn't tell you one good thing about myself. All I knew was what other said, how others felt and their thoughts about me were how I viewed myself. But I finally took my mom and dad's advice "Not everyone's gonna like you! You can do everything in your power to please someone and yet, they will still be unhappy."

Let go of "Still People" People who are still in the same place in life that they were when you met them, stuck at a standstill. People who still blame others for why things are going wrong in THEIR life. People who still are at the same crappy job, complaining, but making no efforts to change or move forward. People who are still with the wrong crowd. People who are still doing the same thing at 25 that they were doing at 15.

We as people need to take control and responsibility for ourselves. We must take that leap of faith, when you have no idea of the outcome but still trust that everything will be fine. On December 11th 2017, I knew that everything was going to be fine. I had made it thru what seemed to be the worst time in my life, and guess what, I'm OK!! A little bumped and bruised but I am stronger today knowing that there are some things totally out of my control. And there are somethings that I have the power to change. (We can't not change the world, unless we change ourselves – Notorious movie) I changed myself, changed my outlook on life and changed my situation by knowing the difference that I am the only thing stopping me from succeeding, I am not defined by my situation.

I had to stop letting people tell me what I could and couldn't do. What I should and shouldn't do. How I should and shouldn't live. Who I should and shouldn't date. I just got tired of people trying to advise me in the direction my life should be going and where I should be at this point in my life. It's my life, so let me live it. I had to start living, and now that I'm living life is so much simpler.

At one point in my life, I thought I had it all figured out. I was in a good space, a very good space actually. So thankful that I was finally in a good space, because I deserved it. Went through so many hardships, it was my time to be happy for things to work out in my favor. They say good things come to those who wait, and boy have I been waiting. I was working at a good job, and when I say good, I mean damn good job. Best job I've probably ever had in all my working years. I was finally able to provide for my kids, pay bills and still live comfortably. It's been a long time since I was able to not stress over where income was coming from. Working and receiving welfare I still was struggling to pay bills. Making just enough money to stay afloat, but never enough for cushion room. Never enough to give my kids the life they deserve. It was times when I broke down and cried ready to give up, because I felt like I failed my children. Yes we had a roof over our heads and food to eat, but just to be able to buy them the latest and greatest of things or just buy them things when they asked for it I couldn't.

I had a man in my life that made me smile. Made me more of a woman, motivated me, excited me, and stimulated me, sexually, psychically, mentally emotionally. I had someone who stood beside me, who led me in the right direction, who loved me flaws and all and accepted me for who I was and who I wasn't.

Although I have a small group of friends, I couldn't have asked for God to have placed any other group of young ladies in my life to be able to experience this journey along with me. It takes a special kind of person to deal with my drama, excitement, bullshit and shenanigans. Some of us may not talk everyday and some I can't escape they asses if I tried, but it's all good, luv is always luv. And I love them from the bottom of my heart. I had established a better relationship, with my mother, and other family members as well. I knew the true definition of home is where the heart is, and family is a solid foundation, and without a steady foundation, I'm an unstable as a baby calf learning to walk for the first time.

I started working out, eating better, and taking care of myself. My hair started growing back, skin started to clear up. I had slimmed down so much. I was at a good weight. I mean yeah, I kinda missed the happy weight, but I wasn't happy with the weight I had put on. I went from a size 20 to a size 13 in less than a year. I had beaten the odds, right when I was ready to give in, something and I know it wasn't anything but God, wouldn't let me give up.

And then one day, I woke the fuck up, and some of the things that I was so blessed to have, seemed like more of a problem some days then a blessing. It was more of an issue and inconvenience then a pro and stepping stone in my life. I tried my best to have a positive outlook on the situation but hey in this lifetime you learn to pray for the best and prepare for the worse, but I don't think I was even ready for the bombshell that was dropped.

Sometimes it blows my mind that here I am in a committed, happy relationship, and I'm still thinking about my payback. How my relationship is going you wouldn't believe me if I told you how hoeish, scandalous, and player I was at one point. Some days I still want my payback, although my boyfriend tells me to let it go, but he doesn't understand. And I'm not sure if you will either. I'm not sure if anyone will ever understand what it's like to never feel good enough in the eyes of someone else. For everything you do and give to put your all into someone and still fall short. to be one of the most loving, caring kind sweet hearted person and to have people take your kindness for weakness and take advantage of you.

Nobody likes being taken advantage of, and me personally, I feel like those who use and abuse people should have a special place in hell.

I remember back in the day getting dogged, getting played, being told I wasn't good enough. I wasn't ready. I'm not tall enough, light enough, I was too thin and then I was too big. I didn't have my shit together, that I was struggling. But aint my God awesome cuz I'm not in that situation anymore. And then same ones who counted me out, I'm now counting them in my inbox, I see them in the streets and they be checking me out. They watching my every move, waiting for my relationship to fail, and thinking they can take Marcus spot. They want what they missed out on wishing they gave me a chance now.

Part of me thinks it's hilarious, like am I not the same bitch that just wasn't good enough? The same bitch you lied too, cheated on, stole from? But now I got a lil ass and you sitting back reminiscing reflecting back on how good the sex was. How I made sure you was straight, never hungry. And then I look at it as disrespect, but I was having fun with it.

I was doing what them niggas was doing. I was making myself relevant. When I thought a dude was moving on, I'd hit em with that "wassup, whatcha doing, how you been, I miss you" text. I'd purposely post a picture that I knew would capture his attention. I'd drive past where I knew he chill at, roll my window done say whats good, sorry I can't stay and pull off.

Now am I wrong? Some say I was, I was acting unlady like, so does that mean that its ok, for a man to do those things because he has a penis, and everyone already has their concept of the way men act. Well tell me this, and if there are any fathers reading this, would you think this would be an acceptable way for someone to treat your daughter, your mother your sister? We are all so quick to talk about Peter Guns, but I know plenty of yall broke asses out here acting like Peter. But when it happens to someone you know and love, yall be ready to take that nigga head off, out here ready to DeBo a mf.

See, now it got you thinking, now everyone wants to try to explain and justify their actions or sit here and try to tell some kind of bullshit ass excuse. Well you can save it. All I can say is, that this is a never ending cycle, when Payton and Kennedi get old enough, I want to sit down and explain to them that there are boys out here who will tell you anything, boys out here who will use you, and mommy isn't saying this to scare you, I'm saying this to prepare you. I want my children to be able to come to me with any and everything, and I know I can't shield them from it all, but I'm going to try with every fiber in my being. I know they'll have stories but I hope not as painful or confusing as mine.

What does it mean to believe in God?

What does it mean to believe in God? As a child I was told God was the highest power of being there was. God was the only one who was able to pass any judgement. He was sin free, God is always watching over you. You think Santa Claus sees everything, well God sees EVERYTHING. Then god saw me stealing, and lying to those I loved and who loved me. God saw the tears my mom was able to hide. God saw the cuts that my long sleeve shirts and pants were able to cover. He saw the bruises make up and concealers were able to make disappear. God knew my struggles, but he also knew my heart. My actions were bad but my intentions were good. God knew my story he was the only one who knew my truth when everyone else knew the lies. I've done a lot of things I'm not proud of, alot of things I wish I could take back or do over. But life doesn't work that way. You don't get do overs you just have to keep going and correct your wrongs.

What does it mean to believe in God? At times I didn't know what the hell that meant. Because I found myself always second guessing, questioning and doubting who he was what it meant to believe in him, and how can someone believe in him when there's so much evil and hatred in the world. How could someone who created the heavens and the earth, men and women both let such destruction happen? He was the same one who help part the red sea, could turn water into wine. Why let your children suffer? I mean I know the whole God and Devil thing. But I've never seen so many things that left me to wonder. I've seen so many fathers taken away from their child so many children taken away from their parents. And I know trust me I know, some of us do the things that put us in that situation but why not give us a second chance?

God was the one who decided who lived and who died, and if this God is so almighty, merciful, humble, and forgiving then why didn't he decide to let Qua live? Why did he decide Qua to be my daughters father if he knew he was going to take him away from her, and the day before hell, two hours to be exact before she was born? I hated God so much for that. I hated the fact Payton and Qua would never know one another. That made me question everything I've ever known everything I ever believed in and stood for. I know everything happens for a reason it's all in Gods time, Gods plan, but tell me what was his purpose why was it his time. And it pissed me off when someone would fix their lips to tell me he's in a better place. I know heaven is the all-time best place to be it's the ultimate goal after life, but I always assumed we'd die of old age.

Don't you think the best place for Qua to be was here? With all the people whom loved him? You mean to tell me that the best place for him wasn't right here, helping me raise our daughter, being able to watch her grow up. So that's a bunch of bullshit, and I truly stand behind that, and I know we are supposed to be forgiving in all, but can I forgive that? Can I? Do I forgive the little bastards that took my daughters father away? How can I forgive when I haven't even had time to heal? When justice hasn't been served? And I have to explain to my daughter that her father isn't here? When she cries out for him, asks where he's at what am I supposed to say? What am I supposed to pray to God, for the answers? Or when I ask what she wants for xmas and she says her dad. Who's going to walk her down the aisle, when there's a father daughter dance and my daughter is fatherless?

I had lost all faith in God a long time ago, when I watched my parent's marriage crumble right before my eyes. The home I knew once filled with such love, and happiness, turned so angry, so hateful and cold. How could the two people I loved the most not love one another anymore. When they said for better or worse? How could God let the worst get the best of them? Til death do them part right? Well neither of them are dead and they still parted ways. God divided my family, allowed them to divide one another, dividing my home. What about the children? What about them, I guess because in my mind, it was no longer about us, what was it in our best interest, was it for the best, or was it they had enough? Was it they gave it all they had and it still wasn't good enough? Did one try harder than the other? Was the love just gone? How does it just leave? My dad was the same man, I remember waking up to every single morning, sitting next to in church every Sunday, was now thousands and thousands of miles away. The only man who I ever loved who ever loved me was the closest thing to me was now the farthest thing from my reach. Our bond now broken. I was raised in a home with both my parents and now to be raised by one or the other. I went back and forth, forth and back from Michigan to New Jersey. The day I arrived was the happiest day for my dad and the day I left I broke his heart. It wasn't fair to him, but it also wasn't fair to me, and selfishly neither one of us understood that. It wasn't as if I didn't love him, or didn't appreciate him but there always felt like something was missing. And I didn't know how to go about saying, all these years I've been hurt, nobody asked me how I felt, or what was it like for me, but not once had I ever asked either one of my parents that.

The same God that allowed me to go from being one of the most loved and straight A student, to the most hated rachettest ass hoodlum going to school with criminals, bad ass, confused ass, misguided ass children. I remember SVRC I still till this day call it baby jail. The step before juvenile. It was mini prison in my eyes. A school with no windows, being monitored to the restrooms, in the heart of the Northside. People got caught slipping all the time walking to and from the bustop. I never was a bad kid, just a little disturbed, misunderstood, I think that what they called it. But I was nothing and nowhere near like the kids in my class. But for some odd reason which actually now seems so realistic and easier to understand and believe, I became a product of my environment. The same kids I once talked about, looked down on and said I was nothing like. I became one of them.

That same God, allowed a child he said he'd protect never leave nor forsake, get taken advantage of. Left me bitter battered, broken destroyed and filled with so much pain and heartache. He kept dealing my hands with players, liars, cheaters, abusers, users, mamas boys hood niggas, and thugs. I thought I found my soulmate at 14. The only other man besides God and my father who knew I thought could ever love me. He knew me, could tell you any and eveything about me. I thought I was in love. Loved him so much, more than I could ever love myself. Thought it would last forever took me on a long and bumpy roller coaster ride off and on for almost 6 and a half years. So why didn't I say I wanted out? Why didn't I let go? Why let someone have the power and control over me for so long? Simple, cuz we accept the love we think we deserve and I couldn't see myself starting over with someone else, giving someone else the opportunity to open me up, know my deepest darkest fears, share my dreams and goals, and didn't they say anything worth having is worth fighting for? Well I was willing to put up one hell of a fight. But after a while, I had nomore fight left in me. When I saw how easily it was for him to move one. I knew as bad as it was going to hurt me to move on, I had to think of myself. I had to stop thinking and telling myself he'd be back, cuz if he left one more time, I don't think my heart could take that kind of rejection anymore.

And just when I thought my heart finally got over that heart break, I met another guy, who had more baggage and problems than the one before. But it was just something about him, something about his smile. Something about him that I thought I could fix. But sometimes even the strongest soliders aren't ready for every battle, and now he's in prison for 23 years. I felt like everything I knew, loved, and wanted was taken from me.

God never showed me no love, no sympathy, no mercy or compassion. I just couldn't catch a damn break.

They say God makes us all in his image, we are all his mater pieces, but I couldn't help but fell when God made me he made a mistake, that he was in a rush that day, was sick and wasn't on his A game or something. God didn't take his time, he made me ugly. And In your head most of you are thinking aww you're not ugly, you're pretty. Giving me the same speeches that I heard all my life, but that's just how I felt. That's what I always felt because that's what I was always told. Always told I was never pretty enough, good enough, nothing. I was just here, just taking up space. My self-esteem was terribly low and I sought for attention and affection from whoever, wherever I could.

I know that there were boys out there who say all the right, real smooth Casanovas, but when you don't feel anything about yourself, anything anyone says will do. When someone comes along selling you dreams, you buy them. Even if it's just for a night, a couple days a couple times a week. Those dreams might drag on for weeks, months, even years. There are some days you snap back into reality and realize you're dealing with a fuck boy, and then he does something to not seem so fuck boyish. That gets you back believing the dreams, believing the lies, believing they love you. Believing they just need time, believing they will change. Believing they gone leave they girlfriend or wife, believing that that's just the baby momma, believing that no one else will or could ever love you the way they do. Believing that it gets better, believing you gotta change yourself just a little bit. You believe all the things they say because you've convinced yourself that it's true. Or you get so tired or afraid of being alone you take whatever you can get. God allowed me to forget my worth; I felt worthless and accepted the love I thought I deserved. I settled and kept settling because I thought that was all I could get.

God was putting more on my plate than I could eat and I couldn't handle it. My emotions were getting the best of me, and had given up. I felt so numb; I was just waiting to exhale. I remember days crying so hard I threw up and kept throwing up, so much that my weight went down. I remember cutting myself because I thought I was better off. I thought everyone else would be better off, hell like anyone would notice if I wasn't here. Who would miss the girl who nobody ever saw anyways??

The same God everyone prayed to, sought out to seek answers from, I couldn't give two fucks about. I thought of God the same way I thought of these niggas. He comes around when he wants too, he answers prayers of those he wanted too, blessed those he saw fit to bless. God went as he pleased he would come and go. The devil was busy with me and I was calling on God to help me, to save me, to let me know that he actually knew I existed but he must had been on another call or wasn't home whenever I called and wasn't getting my messages. It was so hard for me to come to him as humble as I could with a pure heart because I was at a point in my life where I didn't know how, I didn't know where to start. I couldn't repent cuz I didn't know how it had gotten this way in the first place. My life was fuck up after fuck up. is this all my karma? For the lies I've told, thing's I've stolen? Damn, did I really deserve this kind of punishment?

Dear Lord,

Right now I feel like I'm stuck at a crossroads. I need a sense of direction right now I'm so confused don't know if up is really down, if left is right, hell sometimes I gotta look up to the sky to make sure it's really blue. I'm tired, I'm drained and there are days when I want to give up but nothing good comes from giving up but I don't have anymore fight left in me, I'm tired. I feel like all my life I had to fight. When does the fighting stop? I know I gotta stop giving CPR to dead situations, but let me see peoples true intentions, stop sending assholes my way. cuz the way my emotions set up next motherfucker who waste my time, plays me anything of that nature I'm coming for they jugular, spittin in they face making trips to they momma and daddy house. Might have to Catfish they ass, Hell at this rate imma be at 208 S.Harrison in no time just to prove a point.

But I knew that way wasn't working so I had to sit regroup, and rethink on how me and God had been communicating, maybe that's why he was ignoring me. I think I sat for two days in the house, just thinking what was I doing wrong, why were all these things happening to me, so I tried a different way of talking to God.

"God it's Ericka! not sure if you remember me, it's been so long since we last spoke, alot has went on and I've lost faith in you a while back because I blamed you for alot of the things that have been going on. But God, I need you right now things have been going so left, I don't even know what's right anymore. I can't even lie. I was so angry at you. You took everything from me, I never felt more worthless, useless, and purposeless in my life. I look in the mirror and don't even know the girl staring back at me. It's like I know visually she's me, but I don't know that girl anymore. I haven't seen that smile in years. And just when I thought I caught a break it's like sike you gotta be quicker than that. But even with all the bad it's not as bad as it could be. and I'm thankful for that. I know my life isn't perfect but it never honestly will I've spent all these years trying to be perfect when I should have just spent them enjoying and embracing who I am I spent so much time pleasing other people, I forgot about myself, but this is my time, my time, a minor of setbacks but I'm still here, so God I don't know what you got planned but it must be pretty damn interesting.

I was always told growing up, that God answers prayers, and sadly I thought I was going to be able to use that to my advantage. I used to pray for things I wanted, things I thought I wanted and things I needed. Prayed that if God helped me, I'd change my ways. I found myself praying when I thought that it could work in my favor. Now that I'm older I get it. I realized instead of praying for things I want, I should pray for the things I already have. Instead of praying in the midst of things, to pray just because. Don't just pray during things, but pray before, during, and after, I learned to be consistent. Don't stop after things start going your way. I found myself praying for certain people because I thought it was what I should do. I prayed to

God for those who had done things for me, and that karma would get those that hadn't, that, to hurt those in the same way they hurt me. But that wasn't the kind of prayers God answered. So now I pray for forgiveness, for me, to find he strength in my heart to not think of my personal feelings and to be strong enough too understand that if God could forgive those who didn't believe those who questioned him, those who sinned, than who am I to be so heartless, so selfish not to forgive those who hurt me. Everyday, people get hurt, lied too, cheated on, disappointed and as hard as we try to avoid it, we can't. Those are just natural feelings we have. So as I matured I grew older and wiser. I found that although we may want to change the world, we can't change the world until we change ourselves. We can't make the world what we want, because everybody wants something different. The one thing we all have in common is that we all pray. But we all pray for different things, for different people different reasons, under different circumstances. How many of us thank God just because, for no reason at all. Thank God that the sun is shining, that the wind was blowing or that it is raining. We should thank him for the little things, because those very little things make a big difference. So I thank the Lord for waking me up this morning, because sadly not everyone is that lucky. I thank God for my family, and for the little friends I do have because they are the rock that keeps me grounded. I thank him that I have a roof over my head and the food I consume, because not everyone has a home, or food or clothes, and they struggle. Everyday is a struggle. I am thankful because although I don't have much, I do have. My life is not perfect, but I am given the chance to live it the best of my abilities and to learn from my mistakes. (Proverbs 3:5) Trust in the Lord with all your heart and not of your own understanding (Luke 1:37) FOR WITH GOD NOTHING IS IMPOSSIBLE

Call unto him and he shall answer. Well for the longest time I found it so hard to believe this. I found myself calling and praying and begging him to answer me. Psalms 22 " My God, My God why hasth tho forsaken me? Why art tho so far from helping and the words of my roaring" well after days, weeks months, and even years I came to the realization that I wasn't coming to God correctly. I was coming to God with such hate, resentment distrust, confusion and I wasn't speaking Gods words. I would came to God to harm those who harmed me. I wished bad upon those who lied, cheated, and stole. When really I should have been asking for God to help them, and most of all to forgive them. But I was too caught up in my own personal problems, worries and feelings. I thought karma would make me feel better. There times when I used to look in the mirror and wasn't able to were smile. I wasn't able to thank God for what he has given me and blessed me with. I only noticed what God had took, what he let remain broken, what was wrong, wrong with me, my life, and I could only see my flaws and faults. I couldn't see what made me stand out, what made me unique, what made me beautiful.

So what does it mean to believe in God? It means knowing that even though my parents could stop loving one another, they could never stop loving me. At the end of the day although things don't work out, they will always work out in the end. Where there's a will there's a way. And God made a way for both of my parents to be active in my life. Some people have never gotten to even experience what I've gotten the chance to experience. I know love, for my father loved me I saw the twinkle in his eyes when he looked at me and how he's my biggest fan, biggest supporter.

Believing in God means knowing when to just stop, look and listen. I don't know why even still til this day that I thought I had to be a badass, but God was telling me and warning me that, that wasn't me, but if that's the life you want, that's the life you'll get. Thought I could handle it and I cracked under pressure. Me personally it takes a certain kind of kid to live the kind of lives I've seen and now I'm not so quick to judge. Sometimes you have to know the pain to understand their story. And sometimes some kids live the same kind of stories, some live the same kind of endings, leading to nothing but destruction and then you have the kids like me, that may be my situation, but that's not me. My past does not define who I am, what I've been through isn't even compared to the life I'm trying to establish.

To believe in God means, to love who you are even if

nobody else does. There's someone out there who will love you for you. Love everything about you. Have you loving things about yourself you thought you hated. They say in God's time and nobody knows when that is you just have to be patient. I dealt with all these other people till I found the person for me. It was when I had finally given up and said " I guess I'll just be single, I guess I'll just work on myself cuz I can't give my everything to somebody when I haven't given all I have to myself first? You'd be surprised what happens when God sees you trying to better yourself. He will send you someone brings out the best in you. He will bring you someone who loves you as much as he does even without your weave, without the makeup, the money. I'm so happy that I have someone who I don't have to second guess or question. Someone who's not out here making me look like a fool. I'm not just a girl, I'm his girl I'm the only girl. At this time I thought God wanted me to be bitter and lonely when really he wanted me to be better, stronger and happy.

We say God gives his toughest battles to his strongest solider. Well I guess God thought I was built Ford tough. The lessons I've learned and obstacles I've overcame only made me stronger only made me realize its more to life than what people think or watch on tv. Now I don't want you to use my beliefs because this is solely based on my experiences only. It was days when I felt like giving up but I didn't cuz I couldn't. God gives me the strength to keep going. believing in God is after a sleepless night you get you some coffee with a couple scoops of sugar and cream having the attitude to take on the day and get ready to do the same thing tomorrow.

Though, I had given up on God, he hadn't given up on me. He ain't through with me yet. It takes a special kind of person to see your potential and know your worth, even when you can't. It's an amazing feeling knowing that someone has more faith in you then you do yourself or know your capable of. So never give up hope because no matter what your going through it gets better. I promise it does. It only gets better if you are willing to change your circumstances. Don't let circumstances define you! Don't let it hold you back! Everyday I thank God I don't look like what I been through. All I can say is I got through it from being thankful and humble. For what I had and being determined to get not only what I wanted but what I deserved.

So for the last time I ask what does it mean to believe in God? When it seems you're at your lowest point and you've given up, believing in God is giving a mother a piece of her son, a sister apart of herself as well as a part of her brother. Leaving someone here in his absence, giving someone something they lost, a piece of him will live on forever. It was seeing them smile and love Payton that made me feel like the world wasn't ending even with all the bad there's something good. Believing in God means to know there's a light at the end of the tunnel. Believing in God, meant believing in myself and knowing that even when I'm unsure I know that everything is going to be alright. I believe that believing in God means believing in a in a bigger, better higher power believing that you are here for a reason, a purpose, it means having faith that everything's gonna be alright. Believing in God means having faith. Faith is defined as belief with strong conviction; firm belief in something for which there may be no tangible proof; complete trust, confidence, reliance or devotion. The opposite of doubt. Hebrews 11.1 Now faith is the substance of things hoped for, the evidence of things not seen.

I walk by faith and not by sight. It was by me not only having faith but believing in faith that got me through. My faith made a way out of no way, when I thought I ran out of options. faith was what kept me going, faith got me out of bed every morning. Faith was how I made it to where I am today.

See you've got to have faith, you have to have hope and believe. I can't speak for the rest of you all, but if it had not been for the lord on my side, tell me where would I be, where would I be? And where would I be? I have no idea. I look at it like this, all the things that have made me mad, sad, bitter, and broken, but at the end of the day it's made me who I am. Have made me humble, I am a better person because of it. I learned how to love, how to hate. I learned to distance myself from others and get closer to myself.

Ericka

I'm a handful, so get both hands out because I'll keep both your hands full she was different, in every aspect. The kind of girl that not even words could describe. It was something about her that made her special, was it the way she smiled, that made everyone's day brighter? Was it the way she laughed, how cute yet annoying it sounded. She was different, in the sense of being unique, standing out from everybody else? Or maybe it was her ability to love all things as well as people. Though she was a tough cookie to crumble she was still the definition of love. Believed in giving everyone a second chance, even though some didn't deserve it. She always wanted to bring out the best in even the worst people. She wasn't as hard going and ignorant as everybody made her out to be.

People tried to explain and define her character, but there was no one else like her. Her personality was down to earth yet straight to the point. Her attitude, a ticking time bomb, she didn't take no shit. She was determined to be more than what people expected, yet she still wanted that same acceptance from those she could give a damn about. In this lifetime the only acceptance you will ever need is your own. Maybe things would have been much easier if she wasn't so wrapped up in what people had to say.

I came into this crazy world before we knew anything about a recession as Ericka La'Shawn Newman way back when April 9th 1993. Everybody now calls me E-rock because I'm as solid as a rock, no not really, I got my name from this boy name Edrick. Don't get it twisted we are just two people with the same name, different spelling and meaning. I think of myself as the Queen, in my eyes it's all about me. I should be treated like the best. Most people say I'm crazy, psycho, mental, dysfunctional, retarded, funny, forgetful, sassy, a liar, ready to roll, a bit bitchy and my right hand Emoni swears I have short term memory and ADHD.

People have said many things about me, but when describing me all their words sounded the same.

I'm pretty cool calm and collected. There's times when I'm **Entertaining**, **Rowdy**, **Intense**, **Crazy**, **Kiddy** and **Ambitious** but that's just **Ericka**. I love all things and people no matter how ignorant they may be. I take life one step at a time, I learn to live my life and laugh at my flaws. I cry every now and again because it eases my mind and helps me keep my sanity. One thing I'm not is normal, I tried it once and it wasn't for me, it got boring. I'm the best of the worst but what you see is what you get. Don't like it, take a number. I wasn't born to make friends; I was born to make a difference. I smile because life's too short not too.

I was the girl in the back of the class, headphones in ear, chips on the desk, a blue or grape faygo in my lap, and a pack of gum in my pocket, cracking jokes or giving my opinion. I had a one track mind, and it was hard for me to pay attention, especially in math, but I was an honor roll student when I wasn't getting kicked out of school. I had an anger problem, I was one of those kids who used to be angry at the world.

I'm not your average chick, I'm not just ordinary I'm extraordinary and that little extra makes a big difference. I'm not perfect but there's some parts of me that's pretty awesome if I do say so myself. I have the cutest smile and when you look into my eyes you can get lost in translation. I don't confuse hate with jealousy. I might act dumb at time but best believe my momma ain't raise no fool. I'm the worst of the best and the best of the worst. I'm old enough to know better, I'm just too young to care. I guess you can say I'm young, wild and free. I live for today because in this life, I learned tomorrow isn't always promised.

You should always hope for the best but prepare for the worst, so get ready cuz here I come. Boys are like parking spaces all the good ones are taken, but there's always that one that seems so far but is worth it. Just because I hold a conversation doesn't make us friends, and just because I speak doesn't mean I like you. Middle fingers are famous, sadly everybody has one.

I tell people that E-rock is my alter ego. She's everything that Ericka is not. E-rock was strong, defensive, fearless, and never gave a damn about nothing or nobody but herself. She would do what she had to do to get by though at times she did hurt those she loved. E-rock's been shot at, stabbed, bitten, and beat with a lock, burned by cigarettes, choked, spat on and jumped. Sometimes it never amazed me but then again I'm surprised that she wasn't lying in some hospital bed because she had one hell of an attitude. If she had something to say she was going to say it, she said what she meant and meant what she said, there was no biting her tongue and what you see is what you get with her. "I rather you hate me for being who I am rather than you loving me for being someone I'm not and it's more than likely your still going to hate me so I rather you hate E-rock for being E-rock rather than being who you want her to be."

She was like a stain that ruins a perfectly good shirt, No matter how many times you wash it, that stain isn't going anywhere. So every time you where that shirt I know you're thinking of me. I tell people all the time I'm not mean; I just could care less. It's not that I don't care what people think, but I don't value or opinion anymore. I've heard it all, seen it all, been there and done that. So when it seems like I'm cold hearted just think of it as me being real.

So stick that in your juice box and suck it.

Boys love that I'm sweet, but I'm not afraid to be a "bitch" when needed. I don't really do drama, try my best to avoid it. Though I used to be a little rough neck I know how to be a lady and I don't stoop down to any other chick's level. Not trying to sound cocky but that's beneath me.

Boys love that I calmed down and now I be on my chill. That all I want to do is be laid back. Just have fun and avoid petty ass bullshit because I don't have the time or the patience.

Boys loved that I was soft spoken, but I always spoke my mind.

I got, what men, search high and low, over, will fight till the death over, I got the one thing that holds the key, one thing that every woman has, but not all use it to their full potential. The best feeling in the world, to know that good, good. Boys say they respect it, adore it, and would do anything for it. A mind is a terrible thing to waste

They respect when I tell them I'm a lover not a fighter, but I fight for what I believe in as well as love. I ain't gone fight over no piece of dick, cuz if the boy wanted me he wouldn't be talking to someone else in the first place.

One thing that not only just boys love but everybody loved that I was real, and one of a kind. I don't care to be like everybody else, I love being me now that I see that being the same doesn't make us special. Liym told me, "You may not be the cutest girl, but you are one of the realest." At first I took offense to it like he was calling me ugly or something, but that was one of the biggest, and most meaningful compliments someone has ever given me. I don't have to be the prettiest thing out, because looks don't last forever, but the things we say and our actions are our everlasting mark we leave on the world. I don't care to be like everybody else, I love being me now that I see that being the same doesn't make us special.

Boys love that I'm soft spoken, but I always speak my mind.

One thing I don't trust is anybody with my words, because you don't find anybody now a days who can tell a story the right way. I learned my lessons a many of times I never thought I'd have to watch what I say around anybody. I speak my mind and yes I say things I shouldn't but hey that's just me. I have this philosophy if you didn't hear it from me I didn't say it. If you asked me what did so and so say I wouldn't be able to tell you the whole story, I'd add my own things too it not even purposely.

When much is given much is expected. When someone has a certain way they think you should be they expect you to live up to that expectation. But I don't live up to anyone's expectations but my own. Yes, I have high hopes, dreams and goals. I want to be somebody but just not that somebody you may want me to be. Yes I know I have a lot of people who want to see me succeed but they want me to go down their path, but I want to find my own. Go down my own road and write my own life story. I refuse to let anyone tell me who I am or what I am capable of being. Just because people don't like me won't make me change. I know who I am and most of all I know who I want to be. I know that I'm my worst enemy, my biggest fear and threat. I smile even though I'm sad because I'm strong and I never show weakness. Having someone to define you means that you aren't sure about who you are your damn self. That you need someone to tell you that you look good in order to feel pretty that someone has to be with you for you to feel loved. Then again I'm just like everyone else who wants someone to love them, I want to be loved and give love in return. I want someone to hold me, kiss me and just be there through thick and thin. But I can't love anyone until I start loving myself.

I shall only fear God and not man. Matthew 7 says "Judge not that ye not be judged. For with what judgment ye judge ye shall be judged with." The judgment I pass upon you God will judge me with that same judgment. I don't hold grudges. There's nothing for me to hold a grudge against. People do things to us all the time. People have upset me, hurt me, lied to me, and cheated on me. To keep my sanity and God's grace and mercy I forgive them, not for their sake but mine. When they hurt me I pray. I know I may not fully forgive them but I can go on with my day without dirty looks. The power of love changes the way we feel. If you show love others may pass it on.

"I never said I was no angel, nor Holy like the Virgin Mary."-Sistah Souljah

What I am is human, I make mistakes and do wrong things because I'm not perfect. I rather say how I feel then say things in the pleasing of others. I rather you hate me for who I am then love me for who I am not. I rather you respect me than accept me. Acceptance is for pussies, people who don't care about anything and settle for less. Respect lets you know you're on top of your game and got these haters watching.

Beneath all of this strength lies some insecurities. Sadly I'm the type of person that pushes people away and then get mad at them for leaving. A while ago I wasn't happy with who I was. I used to hate waking up being in my skin. I had weight issues and acne. People called me ashtray and ink blot. I had contacts even died my hair to change who I was, because for some reason or another I wasn't comfortable. I hid behind those fake eyes so no one could see into the real me, because I didn't know what or who that was. I did a lot of things out of trying to fit in. I even got a tattoo since I seen everyone else had one. I rushed into it so fast I didn't even make my tattoo have any meaning. There were days when I was hiding from the one thing that would follow me forever myself. I didn't understand that I couldn't run away from who I was. I stopped being Ericka to become New New, New New wasn't working and Crazy E came into place. I hated the image Crazy E had and that's when E-rock came along. I stuck with her for so long because it was just too difficult changing again.

All my life I was told that I wasn't normal, that I

wasn't pretty enough, that I was too dark, too short and weighed too much for my age. It didn't bother me that people called me dark it bothered me most that I was looked down upon and thought of less as a person. The overweight part is was hit me the hardest. I was never told to watch what I eat or was taught about calories and fatty foods. In the Spring of 2010 I looked in the mirror and after hearing all of the you look pregnant jokes I began to wonder was I really overweight. I was seventeen weighing about 166. Was it I weighed too much or that my peers just weighed too little? Was it normal to be less than 130 at my age? Where I come from girls had shape, I guess you can call it extra baggage or more to love. I've never met a girl who weighed 103 pounds and a size 4 until I came to Jersey.

When I looked in the mirror, I hated the reflection staring back at me. I never felt confident. It was like I was in a room full of beautiful people and had no idea why I was in the same room. When people called me ugly I would act like it didn't bother me, like I was made of some type of insult armor, when in reality I would go home and cry myself to sleep. I would pray to God every day that if he loved me so much why he would have made me look the way I did. I would see that everybody was being complimented and would just walk by, and think "damn what I wouldn't do to be that girl. Why couldn't I be born with pretty traits and genes? Why did I have to be the ugly duckling?"

I want you to know just how beautiful you are

Every girl should be called gorgeous even if she isn't. I think that people shouldn't be so worried about the way people look, because even though some people may say it doesn't bother them, it does. Every girl should feel pretty. I don't believe in other people making me feel better about myself, but day after day hear that you're ugly and aren't pretty really has its effects on you. Not saying that I rely on the compliments of others, but damn is it so hard to be nice? I used to wish someone would walk past me, and just say, Ericka you look pretty. That gives girls that extra feeling, that feeling, that no word could describe. When we look in the mirror, everyone see's different images of themselves.

When I look in the mirror what do I see, a beautiful I can't believe it's me. 5'6 luscious thigh and curvy hips, chinky eyes and well glossed lips she looks confident so strong so intense so brave, she like the candy that all these niggas crave

But then I do a 360 and what do I see a low self-esteem teen that looks exactly like me. Teeth in need of braces eyes that can't see a thing, All I see is weakness and I see tears begin to fall I look in the mirror and not a once of pretty at all. I do one more 360 and I then see a smile, that such thing I haven't seen in a while, I'm only as confident as I want as I make myself out to be and only as beautiful as I feel.

This is why so many young girls have self-esteem issues, why so many young girls have eating disorders or commit suicide. Our words are the impressions of us that we leave on the world. I'm not telling you to just go around telling people that they're pretty, but you don't have to go around and tell someone that they are ugly. God made us all in his own image, he made no two people alike.

When I was younger, I wanted to be famous, and now I just want to be loved. My sister expressed that they are the same thing. Both require the attention, affection, and notice of others.

Growing up I didn't want to be black. It wasn't that I hated the color of my skin it was just I didn't know what it meant to be black or live up to a black persons expectations. I saw that the little white kids got to yell at their parents and get whatever they wanted but no not in my household. When I got outta line my mother or father was there to correct me. There was no thinking your high and mighty, and that I should always remember where I came from. But where was it I had come from? I came from a home of humility, and to know that no matter what family comes first. To never let anybody tell me that I wasn't good enough, and that I could do whatever I put my mind too. Black people tend to be loud, ignorant and feel as if the world owes them something, always complaining about how hard they have I, or so I've heard. But I feel as if everyone complains about how the world is treating them. And

I didn't want to be one of those people.

Whatever I set I put my mind to it. Not to prove others that I could do it but to prove it to myself. I challenge myself at every task but it gives me a sense of fulfillment. There are times when I don't think that I can do it but I remember I have a goal and a plan and a story to tell. Any story is worth telling no matter how difficult and hard. When you express what your feeling others can understand you. My biggest threat and deepest fear is myself. I'm my worst enemy and the one challenge that I have overcame. I come to a lot of road blocks because when I face reality I turn and run away. You can't run away from yourself. Stand tall and kick fear out of your vocabulary. So what do you do when you look in the mirror and don't know who or what you are seeing? I turn and walk away and say this image is only what I make it. If I see failure I will fail, if I don't have faith I won't be successful.

Some days I sit in a room by myself and just think. Think about where I was, where I am now and where I want to be from here on out. I think about the friends I've lost as well as those I've gained. I get high in order to balance out my lows to be right where I wanna be. I realized I don't have to be loud to be heard. What you hear about me may be true but you'd never know unless you got to know me. Think what you want but I have nothing to prove to you. This is me point, blank, period. In the flesh, that's a fact end of story, don't like it go fuck yourself. I am who I am but there's always room for improvement. You may or may not have heard of me but by the end of it all I bet you'll have a better understanding of who I am and where I come from. You may not remember me but I doubt you'll ever forget what Ericka La'Shawn Newman stood for. I'm not as different as people thought you'll all soon realize I'm just like you. I have feelings and most of all I have something to say and got damn it I'm gonna say it.

I have a lot of issues if you haven't noticed by now, but it's those very issues that have made me who I am today. I don't regret the things I've done, only the things I didn't do when I had the chance. I have an open heart because love is something that everyone not only wants but needs. Underneath all my toughness is a very loving and compassionate girl. I may not be the prettiest girl, but what I am is real, and it's hard to find girls like me.

Who Am I?

I haven't discovered who I am because I'm now uncovering who I want to be. The only thing I want out of life is to have a sense of completion. I want to say that I made it through the darkest time of my life. I see a light at the end of the tunnel. All I want is to be happy, a not some fairy tale happy you see in the movies. That real happiness that everyday people go through and have. I thought I was different because I hadn't come across it, I didn't notice that it was right in front of my face. I have not the perfect life but it's as good as it gets. I'm just a girl who loves with every inch, a girl who does anything for those she loves.

One thing I know for sure I'll leave this Earth the same way I entered it, with nothing. The only difference this time instead of coming into the world dumfounded I'll leave with more than I came in with. I would have impacted a generation before and after my time. I would have been a mother and wife and did all the things I could have only hoped to accomplish in my dreams. I had dreams a long time ago and sadly each and every dream I've ever had have been crushed. By people who I respected and depended on, people I never once thought would pull be down because I was going somewhere. I used to smile and my smile was broken along with my spirit. When niggas see that you got something going for you they break you.

Every girl has a dream, she has the right to dream. Don't take that dream or crush that dream, because every girl has the choice to make that dream into a reality.

I was easily broken and I was targeted because I was special, I wasn't like every teenager my age. I wasn't involved let alone interested in sex. My parents supplied all my needs and I was never angry. I had no complaints and my house was a home. My main attraction was dolls and candy. That all changed back in September of 2002. My mom, my sister and I packed up and left the only home any of us had ever known. I was in shock and disbelief and tears filled my eyes. That was the first time I cried and knew for damn sure it wouldn't be my last. I was so confused thinking to myself praying to God why my family? From that moment on what I've known was forgotten and never brought back to my attention. I never smiled a real smile ever again. It took every inch in my body to smile to show my mom that I was strong. To let her know that every decision she made was for the best. I couldn't doubt or question what my mother did because she had my best interest at heart me and my sister. Latrice was the only sister I had at that point. She was the only one that I could trust because we was in this together

Advice was something I could always give. When the kids were having trouble I would offer to help. Momma always told me that you can't help everyone, trying to help leads to a road of destruction. Trying to please one person might just piss three people off in the process. Now that, I'm older, I know you can't please everybody, know yourself know your worth. Do what you love and makes you happy. Now don't think I'm not saying don't do things for others, but some people are just low down and un fucking grateful. I didn't listen, hell till this day I never listened to my momma maybe if I would have listened a lot of my problems would have been avoided. I lost lots of friends due to my loving and tender nature but that never stopped me. My niceness was my weakness and it was controlling me each and everyday. One thing I can do is write, and ease everyone else's pain except for my own.

I was easily broken because I never experienced heartache and pain. I never knew what it was like to be called a bitch, now I can't catch a break every time I turn around someone was calling me a bitch. It was the worst kind of feeling for a twelve year old to go through when she was raised around children who weren't angry. I didn't know what a bitch was but if he was going to call me that I would give him a reason to. So I cut out the nice girl act, and became like the girls in my class. I changed my appearance and worked on my speech got rid of the ponytails. I stopped that smiling and speaking to everyone, stopped giving a damn. I should have always given a damn, because no one else gives a damn about me. I realized that I'm my one and only friend, my true friend.

Who Am I? I am the only one who can define that question, I can be anything and anybody I set myself up to be.

If you really knew me, you'd know my house is no longer a home, we who once were united are now broken and divided. There are times when I'm lost with no direction looking for some kind of light, but I never find it so I'm stuck. I never been one to say how real I am I just show it, I am the same way today that I'll be next week, I've seen a lot of shit and done even more. I've been out in these streets since I was 12 so you would think I know how this game is played but it gets the best of me each time. Like every girl all I wanted was love, and I didn't want to be alone, and way back when I was a young girl I would have done anything to have someone by my side, even if that meant settling for less, settling for second, creepin and keeping it on the hush. But I grew up and out of that shit, cuz if I gotta creep you aint worth it.

Some say I have too many standards but that's not it at all, I just have expectations that need to be met, I can't be the other girl, I can't have sex with you at someone else's house, I refuse to let you treat me like shit like some smut or a hoe. I have a name and that's how you address me, don't just use me, because I'm not some bitch around with some good pussy just waiting for you. I want a friend someone who calls to say hi, how you doing? Someone I can hold a conversation with. I want to be taken seriously I don't want you to like only what you see, I want you to get deeper beyond the surface. I want you to be able to make me smile, I want to feel good without a touch, I want to know you love me and not just hear you say it.

Yes I am a bitch, but life made me this way, the people have made me this way, because believe it or not I used to be so nice, so sweet and compassionate I used to smile all the time. But my life isn't all sugar and driving miss daisy, I live real shit, I've been stabbed and jumped bet with a lock by bitches I once trusted, so now I don't trust to many, I look at it this way Karmas one bad bitch and what goes around comes around. People have underestimated me, and used me for the last time. To me trust, isn't something that should be entitled to everyone, trust is something you must earn it shouldn't be handed out like free samples. When you are too trusting people won't take you seriously, it's not that I don't mind a good laugh but not at my expense and stupidity, I don't mind jokes as long as I'm not the one who the jokes on.

I used to be the other bitch, and now I'm that bitch and all the other bitches mad. I used to be that girl that only dreamed. Telling myself, I was grown, and didn't need anybody for anything. Now I'm a college girl, working two jobs, doing for myself, the girls that I wanted to be are looking up to me. Smiling is not only the best reward but the best revenge. These bitches hate to see me doing good so every day I remind them. There's no need to throw it in their faces, each and every day my actions prove why I have no desire to be like them anymore. The "in girls, those popular girls" what were they doing still at home talking about how good the high school years were. Their living out the name they made in high school and I'm making a name for myself, doing what I have to do for myself, because no one else is going to do it for me.

Where I Come From

I come from a place where you smiled even when you were sad, you never showed any signs of weakness, because in this life only the strong survive and the weak get stepped upon.

I come from a place where even though it's dark you have hope in your heart that the light is somewhere at the end of the tunnel. You walk and walk, crawl, stumble and fall, you keep going even if your feet are bleeding. You keep striving and you'll get there eventually.

I come from long days and even longer nights. Hot summers and cold winters. When you felt like giving up you didn't because you didn't want to prove those right who said you couldn't.

I come from a home where my mother worked her

ass off, and never complained. She taught me to rely on myself. I was always told that nobody can do what you can do for yourself, why have someone do what you can do. But now I realize you can't always go at life like that, because you're going to need help somewhere, someday.

I come from a place where dreams were just that, a dream. And I needed to get my head out the clouds and come back down to reality. You can't always have your cake and eat it too. That's just selfish.

Nobody was going to give you anything. Anything you wanted you had to work for it and work very hard for it, you literally had to earn it, and you better not complained because these are the things in life you are supposed to be doing. Always thought you are not rewarded for the things you're supposed to be doing. Like getting good grades in school, not getting suspended, graduating, going to college. All things that in life are supposed to be done, you finish school so you can get a degree, when you get the degree you get better jobs, better jobs equals more money and with money you can do whatever the hell you wanted.

But there were times when you wanted to say fuck it, throw your hands up and yell I give up! because it seemed as if life and everything else was against you. it seemed while you were working so hard other people were just getting shit handed to them. and it made you bitter it mad you hateful and angry, ready to go steal and kill for what you wanted. but in those moments I don't know about the rest of ya'll but I don't look good in orange, I don't want a jumpsuit with a number which some other dirty pussy bitch might have had on before me. i refuse to not wear weave, I don't like being told what to do, how to move, I like being free, i love my freedom, so I never committed any harsh crimes because I knew jail was not the place for me.

I come from a house that used to be a home, where all I hear is yelling. What happened to the love, the smiles? What happened to for better or worse? I guess the worse got the best of them. I've seen hate over power and consume people and turn them into the nasticst, bitterest people that ever walked the face of this earth.

I come from a place where I was told sex is sacred, you don't just do it because you can. I was told sex was something too people did too express their love for one another. And if you have sex and aren't ready sex ruins everything and it does. Sex is nothing but trouble because now a days we use it to escape, to be free, to rebel and just to have a good feeling.

But now we live in a time where sex is just a word, it's a verb or adverb whichever one means something you do, lmao. people having sex just to be having it, because they can, and they want too, Now adays you ask for a condom and the other party gets offended, when I remember back then if you didn't have it they felt like you thought they were some type of scandalous whore, well I guess it's alot of us janky scandalous up to no good bitches around.

I come from a place where family is everything, and without them I'm nothing. I'm only as strong as the people who support me. Sitting at the dinner table is where the magic happened. Bonds were built and where conversations started.

But what happens when you find yourself sitting at the table alone? You learn to depend on yourself because if you wait for what somebody else brings to the table you'll starve. Stop worrying about what others can bring and worry about what you can provide. Now a days people are so concerned what others bring to the table, the may find themselves forgetting, that they are the ones providing the table itself, plates sliver wear and even the food. But we are so obsessed with having someone sit along with us so we aren't sitting alone, even if the person sitting there contributes nothing.

Sad to say we are so invested about what others can do for us, and how useful and beneficial they are to us, we forget how important it is to rely on ourselves.

I come from a place where you use people to get what you want, but feel played when others sell the very same dream we were trying to get them to purchase.

I come from a mind set that you protect those you love. You stand up for what you believe in and always hold your ground. I remember being told never let another nigga break me. People will pull you down like crabs in a barrel but you just keep on going and you'll get out that barrel. Don't be like everybody else, don't stand up for what they think is right but what I believe is right. The moment you start standing up for other people's beliefs is the moment you'll stand up for anything

I come from a household that was told to always have the fear of God. Grew up in the house of the Lord, and as I got older got lost in the world. I was so focused on everything and everybody else and forgot about God.

I come from a mindset where you look out for only yourself. Nobody cares if you succeed. All you have in this world is yourself, your word, your dignity, self respect and pride.

I come from a time, in this generation, as young black woman, we are told were not allowed to complain, we cant be tired, there's no such thing as anxiety or depression, that's a white man's illness. We are taught to be strong, to suck it up and it will be just fine.

But what happens when it's not just fine? When you can't tell when you're up or down? Can't distinguish if you're coming or going, can't tell the difference of left or right? What do you do when you don't recollect the reflection starring back at you? I always thought any sort of craziness had to be a white man's illness, hell they the ones shooting up movie theaters, schools, churches, rally's, all that!

But what do you call a everyday illness the type of illness that forbidden to talk about in most households, so you have to suffer in silence? Does that do more harm than good? How do you get better, if you never get help, how can they help treat you when everyone is telling you there's nothing wrong? I suffered for to long, I went days when I felt like todays the day, I wanna die, today is the day im gonna die, today I cant do it, I'm just tired, I'm not good enough today, today was the day full of regrets, hate and self-incrimination. I had a lot of todays, today could have lasted hours, days or weeks, never knew the type of person you were going to encounter, and I just prayed today wasn't the day. I lost a lot of friends, and good relationships over today, but I keep trying to tell myself that TOMORROW will be better, anything is better than how I'm feeling today.

I come from a place that's barely on the map. Nobody's heard of it and the people who live there wanna get out. And though I left part of me wants to go back. That's where I grew up, learned my life long lessons, that's where my family is, where my heart is and most of all it's my comfort zone.

Where I come from a place that you'll never understand. A place you can't even imagine, not even if I painted the most vivid picture. A place you hear about but doesn't even know it exists.

Nevaeh Watson

So before you guys start thinking, that I might be some terrible, horrible, sick, psychotic ass person who has no life and is going to hell for Catfishing her God brother if you don't already, let me tell you, "This is a story all about how my life got twisted upside down" (In my phresh prince of Bel-Air voice) Let me attempt or try to allow you to understand my logic behind all the madness.

You and probably everybody else has the same question that Nev and Max had been asking, Who the hell was I to go seeking justice? who was I to decide who gets punished and who lives gets destroyed by the lies I told? So who did I think I was? I was the same girl who had her time wasted by the lies and false intentions these so called boys i victimized expressed. If a relationship wasn't something you wanted to pursue then why carry on and pillow talk the situation? i was that very same girl who these boys texted and talked to almost every night and they still couldn't even recognize my voice or realize that all the things? Nevaeh said should have sounded familiar because they were the same feelings that Ericka had expressed. Or was it that they were so caught up in their dog ways they don't noticed these things, because I know I would. The concern and passion I expressed, listening to their dreams, goals, fears, ideas, past all that was real. Nothing about that was fake. So why couldn't they have accepted me for me and not for what they saw or couldn't see past. Why couldn't they try and build with me, see a future with me? they were so quick to thank Nevaeh for helping them see their full potential, making them want to become better people, better men, friends, and fathers, when really Nevaeh was just a mind thing, a figment of the imagination, she was honestly whatever you wanted her to be, she was perfection. Like the alter ego some of us have. She was just a friend who gave the best advice she could, but they say we fall in love based off what we see and then how we feel. So you mean to tell me because she was a pretty face light skin standing at 5'9 straight teeth smile that could brighten up any room. they type of woman Drake described when he said "Sweat pants hair tied chillen with no make up on, that's when you're the prettiest I hope that you don't take it wrong" Nevaeh was the type of woman men could only dream about. the type of girl you'd jacked off in the bathroom too, because she was too good to be true. And usually when somethings too good to be true, it is.

All my life I was told the truth shall set you free. that it should feel good to tell the truth. that its better living in the truth rather than living in a lie. Well if it's so good to tell the truth then why do I feel so bad about it. Why did i get so much backlash? why was it so much easier to live with or hide behind a lie then be honest? why does it hurt so bad? From 2011 to 2015 early 2016 it felt like everything and everybody i came in contact with was a lie. People asked me how could i walk around smiling pretending that everything was ok, still around those same people who had hurt me, and my response was, what goes around comes around, if they can live like nothing's wrong or ever happened well so could I. Hell, people do it everyday. Like those unhappy married couples pretending to be happy. Or the woman who hides her scars behind the makeup. Like a mother who needs a damn break before she snaps, ready to give up and shut down and just say fuck it. But you'll never know it. As women we tend to hide our emotion bottle up what we are feeling and continue on with our everyday lives. But little do we realize all were doing by bottling it up is making the eruption worse. Think of a soda that you shake, as long as its unopened it seems harmless, but the moment you crack it on BOW POW THERE GOES THE DYNOMITE!! and at that point in time, that was me, I had spent some years, bottling up and covering up pain, rejection, unwantedness, embarrassment, shame, and guilt. Hell these niggas had me thinking feelings i never knew i had. Its like when u hear and Adele song or that classical sentimental Drake and Trey Songz. I went thru almost every stage of expressions there was. Deep down don't ever think that I was just going to let that shit slide, nobody's ever off the hook that easy, because I don't like my feelings played with and time wasted, so it's all good. The whole world is built on lies, on dishonesty and misconception. It's our job to weed out the bad apples from the good ones. people only do what you allow them to? so it had me thinking am I gullible? did I bring all this upon myself. No people shouldn't think its ok to use and abuse others, because you never know how someone's mental state is. if these very same people could wrong me, and smile in my face as if nothing was wrong then why couldn't I? why couldn't I give them the same dose of their deadly poison, play the same game they were, but see me I just played it better. I played it a little smarter, and a little harder. someone once told me it's not that we apologize because we are sorry, its because we got caught. if you could commit the very same crime without being caught, would you be sorry, would you still ask for forgiveness? or would you continue knowing that no one knows your secret? Think about that for a second and let that soak in. Now answer honestly would you be sorry? or would you progress into different crimes? Now maybe at least 90% of you all think like me, and wouldn't be sorry, and that's ok, cause I honestly respect that. and feel like that normal. We only feel guilty once we get caught but while you were committing those acts you never once thought about the hurt or pain you were about to cause because you were only thinking of yourself. Maybe that makes me crazy for living my entire life with this point of logic, but I don't apologize for what I've done because, I did it, I meant to do it, and I feel like saying sorry, only pours salt in the wounds and it's not genuine. I made the decision and they are decisions that I have to live with right or wrong. the only thing I am sorry for is letting a bad situation get worse. I'm sorry that I want mature enough to tell that person who I felt wronged me that I was upset and I was hurt.

I am sorry that I wasn't strong enough to let go, I'm not sorry for them, I'm even more sorry for myself. Sorry I let someone have that much control and power to even drive me to this point. I always thought of myself as being strong, but when it comes to certain people I've never been weaker. I am sorry, sorry that I wasted so many years trying to prove a point, when I could have been spending those years investing time with someone who gave a damn about me. I'm sorry to all the young men i never gave a chance because I was so caught up on getting my get back. I wasn't even paying people attention anymore. I was so wrapped up in my own sick and twisted games. in my mind I didn't know who was genuine and who was going to be Nevaeh's next target. In my eyes everyone was guilty, every nigga was the same and deserved the same kind of treatment.

When I was Nevaeh I had the power, the ball was always in my court. and I liked having that control. I liked being the one who decided if I wanted to continue the conversation with these boys, if I didn't want to pick up the phone to talk or text I didn't have to and to see them respond in such a way that they were worried made me smile. but then i had to remember it wasn't Ericka they were trying to get into contact with it was Nevaeh. So when they ask me do I have any regrets, in my mind personally, no I don't. I don't think that I should have been going around being a vidulatntee but then again, who was going to tach these boys a lesson. how else would they know how getting played being hurt lied to and deceived felt? I shouldn't have been trying to be captain save a hoe, trying to cure the world of all the corrupt and evil intentions that men have. but I just couldn't stand seeing these young boys being dogs, I always wondered did they parents raise them that way or did they just not care. I believe nothing hurts more than being lied too! Because you feel shitty knowing you weren't worth the truth. I'm not a bad person, never have been, anybody knows me knows I'm actually one of the most loving, compassionate and try my hardest to see the best in people. and for someone to play me waste my time and lie about their intentions, those people eventually get what's coming to them. I said once upon a time in a rap that I did "You played me daddy, and I ain't with that, karmas a bitch and now it's time I get my get back" And I did just that. I promised myself that one day, some day that ii was gonna get my get back and for about 5 years I did. and it felt so good.

It wasn't that I meant to hurt my godbrother, it was just when you have someone in your life who supports you and is there through everything giving you the best advice telling you not to waste your time because you deserve better, your worth more than whatever bullshit a man can dish out, to see that very same person treat another woman the same way you were treated yea I got angry because I felt like he was such a fucking hypocrite. how you be the same person to women that you were telling me to stay away from? as my brother, I knew he loved me and was only looking out for me but it took us years to establish that. And later on you'll read about Edrick, and the roller coaster ride he put me thru, all the lies, tears and years I put into it thinking it could work, when Tae knew all along that i thought of that relationship differently than Edrick. yes, I blamed Tae for years, for not telling me about the other females Edrick dealt with, how could he? So yes, I was hurt, inside I wanted to die, because the first boy i ever loved might have loved me, but not in the right ways. we were young, yes but being young doesn't mean you have to do people wrong. I was bitter, and i wanted to get back at Tae for that. So I introduced him to Nevaeh, I let Tae see what it was like to have someone come into your life, make you smile, laugh overall happy, and just when you thought things were going good, poof she disappears and your left wondering, was it something I did? was it something I said? was I not good enough?

I'm not sure if you guys will ever understand what it's like to give your all to someone and they play with your heart like it's a toy. I'm pretty sure you have had your heart broken by someone you really liked and cared about, but when it happens over and over again, it breaks you down on the inside, it makes you weak, it leaves you open and confused. it makes you think somethings wrong with you. Have you ever been told that your pretty and you have a good heart and are a great person, you're a good friend? and get left for someone who's even more prettier than you? it makes you feel so ugly inside? Leaves you crying asking God what's wrong with me? Why did you make me this way? Or why did you bring them in my life if you were just going to let them leave. Have you ever just wanted to be loved so bad that you took whatever came along even when you knew that, that person was a fucking scum bag?

I used to think that being alone meant that something was wrong with me. That I wasn't good enough, that I wasn't lovable and that nobody wanted me. I thought it was like the worse thing in the world to be alone. but then I got into a relationship and I got so used to being by myself, that when someone came along, I questioned their intentions, motives hell even their feelings. wondering why me? out of all the people in this world why? what did they see in me? What makes me so special? is their hidden agendas or true intentions? How do I know? Do I continue with this wall I built up, or do I soften up and open up and let them in? I used to be so trusting, open and warm hearted and these niggas turned me into a savage. turned me into someone I didn't even know I could become and I believed I had to hurt them before I could ever give them the chance to hurt me. I had to protect myself, so I treated everyone the same, because in my eyes, everyone was the same. they came in several forms, but deep down they were all the same kind of evil.

But I've come to terms that it's okay to be alone sometimes. Doesn't mean, I'm unlovable, or somethings wrong with me. Hell I been in relationships and still felt alone. Sometimes being alone means being mature enough to take time to get to know yourself because you can get to know anyone else. It's about giving yourself time. time to find out who you are what you like and what your willing to put up and accept out of others. Decide what you want as well as what you need. Being alone means your strong enough to refuse the temptation of thinking you need someone to make you happy. Being by myself was yes one of the scariest and worse feelings ever, but yet it was one of the most successful most meaningful time of my life. I was all about me, I got the chance to focus on my dreams, my goals and aspirations. Felt so good to put myself first and you'd be amazed at what you figure out about yourself when you put in the time. felt great to be able to look in the mirror and accept the reflection staring back at you not having to give that your somebody speech to yourself.

The thing about life, is every one doesn't share the same feelings, goals, ideas and morals as you, but you can't go around trying to make people see things your way. you can't force your beliefs on other people. All you can do is express it, and if they accept or decline that's their choice. and for most of my childhood and teenage years I spend my time trying to make people like me, love me and accept me when really all I had to do was just be me, and if it wasn't good enough for them then move on. but I was so stuck in my ways of having to be liked, having to feel accepted and be right, I wasn't understanding that not everyone is gonna like you accept you or care who you are and how nice of a person you are.

Now I know being Nevaeh gave me a piece of something that I didn't have a long time ago. She gave me a piece of SELF. Self of mind, self worth, and self esteem. Sounds crazy right? Bet you're probably wondering what could I possibly mean. I spent so much time trying to be someone else, I lost my sense of self. I kept on imagining what could people see in her that they couldn't see in me? I forgot the how beautiful i actually was. We spend our years trying to discover, uncover and reveal who we are to others, so others can love us. When really all we can be is ourselves and others can take it or leave it.

I learned so much about self worth through Nevaeh. I learned to know yourself and your worth. Nobody should ever make you feel like who you are isn't good enough. That you need to change to meet someone else's standards. Don't be little yourself trying to raise others up. Nevaeh was the best and worst thing that could have happened to me, she made me bitter, but also made me better. And I thank the boys who broke my heart because instead of listening to sad love songs, feeling sorry for myself, thinking like the Script "She's moved on and I'm steady grieving, cuz when a heart break, no it don't break even! What am I posed to do? When the best part of me was always YOU! And what am I posed to say when im all chocked up and your ok" I used my heartbreak as my stepping stone. I used it as a reminder of what I will never put myself through. I will never allow someone to have that much control over my mind or my heart.

Relationships and Love

No road is long with good company. ~Turkish Proverb
"True love is like a pair of socks: you gotta have two and they've gotta match."
We come to love not by finding a perfect person, but by learning to see an imperfect person perfectly." Sam keen

A good relationship, what makes a relationship good? A strong bond, openness and being able to always tell the truth. You can't be in a relationship with someone who you aren't friends with, someone you aren't close with and don't connect with. Acceptance and never having the feeling of is my flaws going to be a problem. Everyone wants acceptance and not have to worry about being judged. Your partner knows your deepest darkest secrets and won't throw them in your face every chance you get. They see you for you, the love you for who you are even more for who you aren't.

A good relationship has happiness, and encouragement. They smile when you smile and when your sad they'll do whatever it takes to make you smile. They will hold your hand in public and aren't afraid to call you their girl. You have met just about every family member and are invited to just about every family function. A good relationship is built on support, they are there for you when you need them. They are holding your hand telling you not to worry because you're in this together.

A good and stable relationship is based on communication. If you can't hold a conversation with someone you call yourself liking or in love with its gonna go nowhere. Being able to talk to someone about the little things lets them know you care and isn't it the little things that matter? If you talk to someone that you can't talk too, truth is it isn't going to work. I've talked to boys that I could be so open with, there wasn't anything that we couldn't talk about. Then there were boys I found myself just listening to one another breathe, hearing him have side conversations when he was supposed to be on the phone with me.

A boy should never care about your past, because as long as you aren't doing what you used to do it doesn't matter. He or she for that matter shouldn't care about who you been with or what you did. If you feel comfortable talking about the past and they don't past judgment they are a keeper. If you are scared to talk to them about a relationship that didn't work or how you're afraid to trust and open up to someone they aren't the one for you. You don't need to feel pressure from the one you care about. If it doesn't bother you and you are able to move on why can't they?

I had this one boy and what made us last so long was that we were friends before we dated were friends all while we were dating and even after we broke up we remained friends. Friendship is the most important thing in a relationship. I've even had relationships that I was in based upon the fact the only because we were lustful to one another and were sexually attracted to one another. I've been with people who I knew were no good but I wanted to change them or prove to everyone that they are wrong about them.

I'm just a girl who overdoses on love. I fall in love with what we were and became blind in seeing what we were becoming. I second guessed myself a lot of the time. I put up with things because at first I didn't know any better. I opened my heart only to get the door slammed in my face with what we call heartache, heartbreak, deception, and most of all rejection. I never asked for any of this to happen it just did. One day feelings I couldn't explain or couldn't handle came into place and just magically appeared. Love is a constant battle that I'm constantly losing. I thought I'd find my soul mate but I'm too young for all of that. The right one is out there, I just haven't found him or he jus hasn't found me. I looked high and low never in the middle. I found people that liked me for the wrong reasons. Nothing was good enough. Was I even good enough?

I wanted people to see me for the way I saw myself. To go beyond the surface, I want somebody who not only knows me but is still willing to learn. I don't believe in love at first sight, maybe it was all in a matter of what I was seeing. I focused on what wasn't as focusable to others. I always believe that in time all things may get better. I stay because I don't wanna leave and give up.

"You can't hurry love; no you just have to wait. She said love don't come easy it's a game of give and take. You can't hurry love; no you just have to wait. You have to trust give it time no matter how long it takes." The Supremes

Have you ever thought you been in love? Horrible isn't it? It makes you so vulnerable. It opens your chest and it opens up your heart. It gives someone the opportunity to impact your vision, your thoughts, and your emotions, hell your whole life and it means that someone can get inside you and mess you up. You build up all these defenses, you build up a whole suit of armor, so that nothing can hurt you, then one stupid day, one stupid person, no different from any other stupid person, wanders into your stupid life... And things don't seem so stupid anymore. You give them a piece of you, a piece they didn't deserve, a piece they didn't ask for. Then they did something even stupider, like kiss you or smile at you, and then your life isn't your own anymore. It takes a fool to learn that love don't love nobody, it's not love who loves but people who do. People have the control to either hold on and let go. People fall in love, too early without the clear understanding of what love is. Love can be the sweetest feeling, when felt not by sight but of the heart. When it's not real love takes hostages and doesn't care who it hurts in the long run. Leaving something so little so simple into something so big. Leaves you hurting and crying resentful mad, jealous at the next girl. Have you ever been in love? Horrible isn't it?

Each time you fall in love it feels brand new. You love them for their own reasons and never say the same thing you said about the ex. What you see in someone you may see in someone else but in a different way, shape and form. Each time you hug them you feel a different feeling. I felt warmth each time but for a different reason. I don't regret anything about these boys, and I wouldn't change them because it was something about them that attracted me to them in the first place. You never forget that feeling you get when you're near them and more so when you're away.

Maybe that's the problem, we are so easy and willing to love. Why is that? Because everybody wants to be loved. Everybody wants somebody who wants, them someone who accepts them, who values them so they feel complete.

I want

I want someone who will nap with me in the middle of the day. Someone who thinks they love me as much as I love them. Someone who thinks about me as much as I think about them. Someone who tells me forever because he never plans on leaving. Someone who will plant flowers with me in the spring, go swimming with me in the summer, jump in a pile of leaves with me in the fall, and someone who will build a snowman with me in the winter. Someone who will be willing to do it all again with me next year.

I want someone who will ask me how my day was, and really wants to know. No matter how long or boring it was. Someone who will laugh at my jokes even if they aren't funny. Someone who not only values me but respects me. Someone who doesn't care about my past but our future. Someone who will lay on the hill and watch the sunset with me. Someone who holds me with the satisfaction of never letting go. Someone who doesn't break their promises and someone who don't make promises they can't keep.

I want someone who knows random hugs and kisses makes your whole day brighter. Despite their fears will tell me everything not be afraid and trust me. Someone who will never doubt what I have to say. Someone even if he doesn't know he tells me everything will be okay. Someone who knows me but is still willing to learn. Someone who will go the distance, whatever the distance may be. Someone who picks me up from the airport to be the first to see me and, someone who sees me off to be the last to say goodbye.

I want someone who won't disrespect me but will protect me. Someone that treats me good even when I treat him bad. Someone who treats me as an equal and will never underestimate me. Someone who loves me when I'm least deserving of it because that's when I need it the most. Someone that never feels the need to lie and someone who is open because there are no secrets to hide.

Most of all I want someone who wants me for me. Someone who doesn't just tells me they love me but shows me he loves me.

So I ask myself is what I want to much to ask? Should I lower my expectations and just take whatever comes my way? Do I need to get my head out the clouds, is it too far stuck up my ass to realize what's really going on? Is love something that you hope for, must look for, or something that comes along when you least expect it? The part about growing up is understanding what's right in your life, who's right in your life. Growing up you stop thinking about the dumb shit and start thinking on how things will affect you now. I take it as if I never fully grew up, it never dawned on me that the choices I made would have an impact on me later on down the line.

What is love? The dictionary defines love as a noun. A strong affection for another person. I define love as an adjective because it's something you do. To me love is a strong bond and a feeling that never changes. Love:: stands the test of time, never dies or fades away, loves you when your least deserving of it because that's when you need it the most, is there when you act as if you don't give a care if it leaves or stays. Love is everlasting and it is true, and it will always love you no matter what you say or do. So many of us want love but are capable of giving it. We want commitment but aren't willing to commit and settle down. We are expecting of so much but what are we putting forth?

I guess you can say I can go on and on about what I think love is and what it should be. Now I'm going to give you some examples of relationships, simple misconceptions of what I thought love was and how foolish I was.

Am I In Love??

"The more we are filled with thoughts of lust the less we find true romantic love." Douglas Horton Mike Hardcastle says "How can I tell if I'm in love?" What feels like love to one person may not be nothing more than an attraction to another. Some people fall in and out of love quickly, while others often never say there are in love but lust. Lust is a very powerful, very intense feeling of physical attraction towards another person. It is very common for people to confuse lust with love. But why? What is it about lust and love that make them so easy to get mixed up? Lust is the physical attraction and only the physical attraction. If lust is all about sex how can it be a relationship? Without the sex, there is no relationship just relations. Love is much more than physical attraction but inner beauty.

Lust is clearly not love. Love is based on caring, friendship, commitment and trust. Love is a shared feeling between two people who have vested in one another's happiness. Love is not about jealously, love is a positive feeling. Love is the total surrender of your heart to another person with the security of knowing they will do the same, or try and treat you better than even you feel as if you can. Love should feel good not bad, it's should feel wrong, it shouldn't feel wrong, like when you sneak and eat a box of chocolate when you know you're on a diet. Love should make you want to be a better person; it should not lead you to self-destruction.

If it's lust
- Your in love with her body and her body only
- Even before learning her name you are already fanaticizing on what you want to do to and with her.
- you only call her to see if she's available to have sex
- You act as if you really don't know except when you to are all alone.
- She's a booty call,

- You make excuses not to spend time with her, but you make all the time in the world for her when it comes to sex.
- After having sex you look for the easiest way to leave, no cuddling, no breakfast, no I'll call you later, Just a I gotta go.

Some ways you know when your in love.
- When you cant stand being away from that person for too long, there's a difference between spending time and being clingy.
- You cant stop looking in their eyes
- When you feel as if that person has made you a better person in the end.
- Neither of your partners feel the need to test the other's loyalty or feelings.
- your partner asks you to choose between them or your family or friends.
- When money is not a factor, you don't have to go on a date, just being with that person is good enough for you.
- When you feel inspired, like there's nothing you can't do
- Your partner is your rock, your solid foundation, will hold you down till the end, through thick, thin and everything in between.
- No matter how heated the agreements get and how mad you are, you can't stay mad at that person for a very long time.
- All of your self doubt goes out the window with just one look. Being truly in love makes your forget about any insecurity you may have. Makes you respect yourself. Remember you must love yourself before you can love anyone else.
- Love is something you don't have to think about you just know. It's that amazing feeling, that smile on your face even when your having a bad day.
- Laying in their arms makes you forget about all your

troubles and worries, they can wait another day.

- your in love when you can see past their imperfections, you know they are not perfect and those imperfections make her who she is.
- Your in love when you can say without hesitation in your voice and proudly say that your happily taken.
- If you are truly in love there will be no mistaking it. Its so intense and overwhelming you begin to lose yourself. You lose yourself in that someone, now that's love.
- When you know every little thing about them, like their favorite color, day of the week, what they like to drink or eat. When you go to the store and the first thing that comes to mind when you pick up something is oh he or she would love this.
- you have great chemistry
- You get lost in the conversation, the hours pass like minutes. You listen to every and anything they have to say
- Even if you see her at her worst you still think she's beautiful
- Its important for your friends and family to not only meet her but like her and accept her.
- You start doing things you never done, like buy flowers or make dinner, and try to do little sweet things.
- She challenges you and motivates you
- She makes you happy, so you'll do whatever it takes to make her happy.

Love is when you care about someone more than you care about yourself. Lust is when you can't stop thinking about having sex with them. Infatuation is when you can't stop thinking about that someone, your desperate and just have to have them at any cost. Is possible to love someone lust for them and be infatuated with them?

Ask yourself these questions
- Would I be willing to actually spend the rest of my

life with this person?
- Am I willing to let him or her go if I felt it was for the best?
- Am I willing to wait for this person if they aren't ready to have sex?
- If they moved would I still be willing to try or put what we have on paused or just give up?
- What am I really willing to do for this person?
- Are they worth meeting my friends or family?

If you answered no to any of these questions it is a result of lack trust. You are more than likely afraid? It is just a new feeling you are not used to or are you just being selfish?

You can't be afraid to ask what do you mean to him and how does he feel about you and why? Any boy can say I love you, and I think your great, but what is it about you he loves? And what about you makes you a great person? Why do you make him smile and what is it about yourself that made him like you in the first place. Think of how you two relate to one another. How do you communicate if there is any communication at all? Do you argue? And if so how do you deal with the conflict? Do you bring out the good, the bad, or the ugly, in one another. Can you be yourself around that person or do you have to be what they think you should be?

You need to know the difference between, a crush, lust, puppy love, a fling, infatuation, and the real thing. Ask yourself what love is and ask your partner as well to see if they match up. Love might be one of the twenty three things I mentioned and love for him could really be spending time and having sex.

A lot of the time I wasn't able or was incapable of telling the difference. All this time I thought love was just a bond that couldn't be broken, and never ending feeling no matter what happens.

I'm so glad that these events have passed and, I am able to laugh about it now. Looking back asking myself Was I in love? It wasn't necessarily that I was in love. It was the thought of thinking I was in love that kept me happy, that's what kept me going. And now that I'm older and know what I want and what I deserve, I might have truly loved these people as a person, but not the situations that I was in. Donell Jones said, "When you love someone, you just don't treat them bad." And if they love, loved or had any type of love or affection for me they wouldn't have done me like that.

Edrick

"We all grow, it's just that some of us grow apart."

"Because of you I never stand too far from the sidewalk, because of you I learn to play on the safe side so I don't get, Because of you I learned to trust not only me but everyone around me because of you I am afraid." Kelly Clarkson

April 22nd 2008 changed my life forever. I was just Ericka and then I became E-rock. I shouldn't have let those two worlds collide. I should have left it alone. At times I wish I never been introduced. I thank Edrick for everything he's taught me but at this expense no.

I'd never forget the first time I physically met Edrick. This boy kept walking past my street he just looked like a lost puppy that was thirsty according to my Big momma. After hearing my Big momma talk about how he carried himself, I didn't want him walking up to the front step. My mom and Big momma left so I asked excuse me sweetie are you looking for somebody? It was something about Edrick that made him unique. I never dated someone so much taller, slimmer, or older than I. Edrick went against everything I said I would date. That lifestyle he was living wasn't for me. We lived in two separate worlds and I should have never been introduced to his. Psychically I could stand it but emotionally my heart body or mind wasn't ready to bear it.

There was something I couldn't put my finger on. I was scared to trust Edrick, I told him I was afraid of being hurt. I couldn't just give my heart away but I was willing to let Edrick have it. I just felt comfortable talking to him, and never thought that anything would happen. I couldn't figure out why I was able to be so open toosomeone. I never trusted anyone let alone put my trust in someone.

I heard the doorknob twits and knew my mom was home.

There was no way Edrick could get out of the house without my mom seeing him. He was going to have to jump out of the window. Before he jumped I hugged and kissed him, savoring this moment forever. This day was special for the both of us. I stood staring out the window as he ran out the backyard thinking to myself, It's easy for someone to come in but to watch them leave is the hardest thing you have to do.

My dad had come and told me that I was going to stay with him for the summer. I couldn't even feel happy because all I could think about Edrick. My last night in Saginaw I spent it with E-roc with no concerns for tomorrow. I pretended that none of this was happening, that I was just over reacting and it would be over. I had a gut feeling that this relationship wasn't going to work but, he reassured me that I had nothing to worry about. Edrick said that he could ease my mind and have me not worrying about anything other than him. Having sex with him meant everything. We both wanted it, I wanted to have a strong relationship; we needed a strong and stable foundation. I just wanted to hold my own and keep us only moving forward. I wasn't teased or tricked nor provoked. I wanted us to have sex for the right reasons because we were in love and were sure about where we were going.

I knew that night wasn't going to last forever. Sooner or later after I left Edrick would have thoughts about fucking somebody else, I just thought our bond was strong enough to hold him off. To make him remember the commitment he made to me. What was that commitment supposed to be anyway? I didn't even know what a commitment was? A commitment is to entrust another's care and a pledge. The only thing that I wanted him to commit to me was that he would always love me, that even when there were times when we were ready to give up that we'd try. That we could hold off our sexual temptations and always be honest.

Ericka: "I'm so mad at you Edrick"

Edrick: "Why? What I do bae?"

Ericka: "It's not what you did, its what you didn't and haven't done. I don't want to force and have to remind you to call me and be my boyfriend. I don't feel you love me"

Edrick: "Ericka I love you so much, and no other girl can come before you or between us. You wifey, not my boo, my bitch, or my hoe. You wifey you're irreplaceable. I been waitin for you since the day you left me."

Ericka: "Babe I know it's gone be hard, but we can get through this. I wanna be wifey forever, I can't imagine being in any other position than the one I'm playing now."

Edrick: " Girl you can't miss me as much as I miss you so cut it out. Plus you got my heart so I'll always love you."

I couldn't imagine my heart belonging to anyone other than Edrick. I never knew he felt that way. I wanted to keep his heart in a safe place so I kept it next to mine. It was so strange because I got a message from this girl named Sheika. I've never met or heard of this girl until today. She told me that Edrick was talking to this girl named Natasha. Not once did I think of her to be lying, for what purpose? I asked Edrick and he came right out and said that bitch Sheika was lying.

I called the house and his little brother answered, he told me not to call anymore because Edrick had a new girlfriend. I listened to the sound of the dial tone until I got tired of feeling sorry for myself. I was so shocked in puzzled because I just had that conversation with this nigga and he lied.

I think I listened to the dial tone for about twenty minutes. I don't even know why I was so upset. In the back of my mind I knew something was gonna happen but I thought he had enough respect for me to tell me, instead he lied and tried to make it seem like it was no big deal. Acted as if it was my fault that I moved to jersey. Little does he know I would have stayed jus to be with him.

Ericka: "Dude what the hell is your problem? How stupid do you think I am, like I wasn't going to find out? I asked you bout that bitch just last week and what did you say that I was the only one ha, what a load of shit that was."

Edrick: "What did you expect you all the way in New Jersey! I told you I wasn't ready that I couldn't handle long distance."

Ericka: "You really want to know what I expected! Not for you to lie and play me for stupid. I expected the truth, You too damn old to be playen these little kiddy games. Your eighteen and jus because I'm young don't make me no young dummy. I couldn't do this but you told me you would try.."

Edrick: "I still love you. I'll always have love for you. You'll always have a piece of my heart. It just belongs to Tasha now."

Ericka: "You're a fucking liar Edrick, because if you love me, still love me or have ever even loved me, you wouldn't do me this way. I don't deserve that, all I ever did was love you, but I guess my love wasn't enough.

It was supposed to be you, it was you who was supposed to love me, protect me, hold me and it was you who was supposed to be there until the end of time. But yet it was you who left me, hurt me, who was the reason of all of my pain, who broke everything, every promise, and most of all you who broke my heart.

But how? Why? When it was you who made me smile, you who made me laugh, you who kept me safe and warm, you who took away my pains, my doubts, my fears, my worries.

It was you who knew my favorite color, favorite song, and favorite food, you who knew everything about me. And wasn't it you who promised me forever? But forever wasn't everlasting, it was supposed to be you, supposed to be me, supposed to be us. It was supposed to be you, it wasn't supposed to be him, or her, none of them, or any of those other pointless, meaningless relationships. Because those people were just people. People we used, people who occupied our time, people who made things seem much simpler, and easier, and it was those people I used to try to get over you.

It was you who made me believe, it was because of you that I was strong, and because of you that I was weak. It was you, it was supposed to be you whose last name I stole, you who I shared a family and the rest of my life with. But apparently it wasn't me. It wasn't me you wanted to be with, wasn't me you saw forever with. It wasn't me you loved anymore, it wasn't supposed to be you who moved on, who forgot, who didn't care.

I always thought it was supposed to be you, about you, that everything revolved around you, but now it's supposed to be me, me who finds the strength to love again, to find the strength to move on.

Even after all of that I kept in touch with Edrick. It just seemed strange, we didn't talk like we used too. You could hear in my speech that I had something to say, but I swallowed it and kept it in my head. The first time he called me bro I almost had a heart attack. I didn't know what to say or how to think. When I moved back me and Edrick smoked, chilled and finished what we started back in April. I came to realized I wasn't wifey anymore, so who was I stepping down to become his bitch or his boo? Was I really able to live with the fact that I was just some bitch that would be there when Tasha wasn't? I couldn't believe this was happening, he said I was wifey and nobody could or would come above or before me. You shouldn't say things you don't mean. If you can't follow through on your word don't lead me into believing you can. A lot can happen when you tell people things that you don't mean. When you don't have the same intentions as they do, hearts get broken that way. I had sex with Edrick still, I tried to justify it by the fact that I felt safe once upon a time and I didn't want to lose my sense of security or stability. Then again, I justified it by I had no commitments to Natasha, she wasn't my bitch and plus I didn't like her, but wasn't I doing the same thing that she had done to me? Was my ignorance a simple act of revenge? Could I really see myself breaking up a so called happy home? Well what the fuck about my happiness, my home that she destroyed? She didn't care so neither did I. Edrick wasn't mine anymore, he was public, like an outhouse or a bus stop. There was no warmth in knowing that he was mine and only mine, I couldn't help but feel stupid that I was willing to share him.

Edrick: I always wanted to ask u this am i like the only dude that care 4 u and call you more den any one of your other male friends and am i getting the same in return....i asked cuz it seem as if u do got other male friends its jus that i wanted to kno do i get the specialist treatment cuz how me and u is ya kno juss askin???

Ericka: You've always been that guy. Who comes before any other nigga, but lately I just been putting you off, and trying to hide how I feel cuz I knew this was gone happen. That I was gone fall right back where I was in 07. No matter who came along you came first, you've always been here for me and I've been there for you and no new relationship we get into can change that. Cuz I love you Edrick, and nothing and nobody can or will ever change that, when I'm around you I just get to be free, I've never been able to be myself, because who I was, I was never good enough, we've laughed together, cried together, and yet were not together.

Edrick: that was real caring for you to let me kno dat on da real real cuz i was juss wonderin cuz i kno i aint the only guy u fuck wit ya kno

Ericka: yea i kno... just like I know I aint the only girl you fuck with but at least I'm honest about it. But I learned to deal with what I can't control. I love you, and deep down I know you loved me or so I would have hoped it all just wasn't a game because you can't just play with people's feelings heart and emotions. but you're the only one i fucks wit...n any real deal manner.. i just wanna kno is what we have worth waiting for.... do u honesty think we can do three years an make it to four... cuz once my b-day hit..i can do whatever the fuck i want.. and if you still waitn imma keep it tis way forever cuz i lik this us...

Edrick: Well if I am the only one you fucks wit like that, shit we can make anything happen. That's if we both down for it cuz how I feel right now shit im willing to try it out again, but this time we gone have to make it work cuz I really aint trying to be alone again. I hate that feeling of being lonely. But if we was to make it work this time, you gone have to cut all yo lil niggas off on the real, cuz I'll fuck you up bout some shit like that! I know you ain't gone just cut them all off right now, it ain't that easy but we just gone have to see cuz I'm still contemplatin at the same time.

The crazy thing about it all was that I was ready and willing to give any and all of them niggas up for Edrick but was he willing to do the same? I shouldn't make excuses but, I only kept them side dudes around when my so called main one wasn't acting right. But they were just that side dudes, dudes you keep around and are there waiting for you. If they cheat or lie, there's no harm, no foul. What more do you expect from a dude who knows he a side dude cuz you're a side chick to him as well. Time after time, Edrick had proven me right when I said age was nothing but a number, it didn't matter that he was 18 and I was 15 because when it all boiled down, Edrick acted like he was the immature teenager. What was there to contemplate and think about? Either he wanted to be with me or not? I wasn't beat for playing the childish ass games because the one thing that can feel like heaven can also hurt like hell.

I couldn't tell you why I was keeping him around? I wish he would stop being such a dickhead and open his eyes and see what was right in front of his face. I was so caught up in who we were I had no idea who we had become. I still was apart of Edrick regardless of what anyone thought.

Edrick: "Man wassup, when you gone come to the hood cuz I always come to you."

Ericka: "If we continue any longer it's gone stay that way. I don't come to niggas they come to me. Plus you aint my man, if you want it, you gone have to come and get it. I don't need it, nor do I need you!"

Edrick: "Damn girl we like that. I thought we was cooler than the other side of the pillow."

Ericka: "Yea we is but that's all we'll ever be. Imma always have some type of love for you, I cant give up on you that quickly. I can't forget what we had, but there's a limit to what I'm willing to do. I'm not bout to be that bitch in your life, besides what's going on with you and he wifey."

Edrick: "Me and Tasha still together, that's my baby. I had feelings for you but all we did was chill and fuck, so that's all I'm used to with you. We never did anything else"

Ericka: "No you just didn't want to do anything else, but if you're happy then, I'm happy for you."

Edrick: "Yea thanks, we are really happy. I can't make you happy anymore but I can leave you satisfied."

I didn't want the need for satisfaction nor did I want to be second best or settle for less. It's not right I have to hurt while he goes along with his day. It's not right to spit in the one person's face who gave a damn about you. I gave up a lot for Edrick. I should have just stayed a fourteen year old girl who only cared about herself. "He's moved on while I'm still grieving cuz when a heart break it don't break even."- The Script

Our years weren't the strongest years or the best year but regardless they were our years, Years I spent trying to make it work, Years I spent trying to make you understand. What happened to all those smiles? When I looked in your eyes and saw forever. You told me don't be afraid to fall and I wasn't but then something changed. You changed. Now I'm afraid to fall because I'm not sure you'll catch me. I'm afraid that once I get comfortable thinking we have potential you'll get up and walk away. I'm afraid that if I let you won't come back. And if you do you'll walk in and out of my life. How did we make it this long? Was it fate that kept us together...No it's my ability to forgive and forget. To swallow my pride, my hurt, my anger and move on. So I scribble your name out my notebook. Cut all the pictures rip all the letters. And do the hardest thing I ever had to do and that was stop feeling SORRY for myself. Because it's clear to me these years meant nothing to you.

Tasha: "Ericka wanna be E-rock. Bitch why you jockin me an my man you need to get a life. You must aint got one! Just to let you and anybody else know he aint going nowhere."

Ericka: "No aint nobody being petty but you, I could honestly care less about you. Your not the one who I was screwing so what is your purpose."

Tasha: "Damn bitches love my name that's a damn shame. Take my name off your page, no keep it on their because I'm famous."

Ericka: "Yea you gone always be famous, famously

stupid. How do you sound trying to check me on something you know nothing about? On some real deal stuff sweetie, do you think you're the only one Edrick's is having sex with? If so you're wrong. Do you think you the only female he said he ever loved? Nope boo your way outta line talking to me like that. He's happy wit yo raggedy mouth ass so just Imma just leave it alone."

There was a lot I wanted to get my chest. I shouldn't have been telling it to Tasha but she started it. I knew I was being petty but hey, I hate when females jump hype when you need to confront your man on what he's doing. I'm not committed to anyone but myself. Edrick was still willing to be with me and deep down I didn't want to leave, I didn't think I knew how. I wasn't his girl and since that bitch wanted to mess up my relationship why couldn't I mess up hers? Even though I hated Tasha I wanted to know why she hated me. It wasn't like I ever did anything to her.

Ericka: "All jokes aside Tasha what is it you got against me."

Tasha: "When a female in a relationship better yet in love she'd do anything for him. Basically, I gave you a warning and look what you had to say."

Ericka: "No it wasn't what I had to say it was my reaction. You came at me as if I knew about you. It's fucked up cuz you knew E-roc had a girl and continued to talk to him. But how do you think I feel I was in love and willing to do anything for this boy, but I know who I went off on and it wasn't you. Edrick was my boyfriend he was to me what you are now, and I fell as if you stole him from me. It's a shame that you don't understand the shit you started, why would you talk to a boy who you knew had a girlfriend, you should have told him to wait and break up with me then you talk. So I don't feel bad for anything that I've done"

I said she stole him from me but honestly what was it that she stole? You can't steal something if it was already in the process of not being yours. I guess I felt as if she stole him because I had no clue what was going on. It wasn't that she stole him, Edrick was in the process of leaving anyway, it just would have been nice to have a heads up and not been lied too. We based what we had on friendship and trust but he broke all of that. Friends don't lie and hurt their true friends, and he broke my trust when he started becoming distant and lying to me.

We had both been talking to Edrick around the same time, but there was nothing either of us could have done about it. A lot of what I had to say was based on anger, jealousy, confusion, and rage. After talking to Natasha she wasn't as bad as I made her out to be. I realized I can't force someone to love me, if I did it wouldn't true or genuine. I wanted to just forgive and move on, for my own good because hating Edrick or Tasha wasn't going to help me feel better. I was driving myself insane making things harder than they had to be. I was angry and for what? There was nothing I could do and it wasn't as if something was wrong with me. I was mad at the fact that Edrick had a girl and didn't bother to mention it. On the other hand, Tasha already knew and why take something that's not yours? Why be low down and ruin a relationship?

There's no reason to be low down other than the fact that you can and because you can most girls will. Lawrence DurDale said "It is not love that is blind but jealousy" and it is. We go after that person we are seeking for the wrong reasons. Jealously is nothing more than the fear of being abandoned and envy. "Love" is that condition in which the happiness of another person is essential to your own... Jealousy is a disease, love is a healthy condition. The immature mind often mistakes one for the other, or assumes that the greater the love, the greater the jealousy. **Robert A. Heinlein**

I had to be the bigger person and not be childish anymore. I hated the tension and bad blood. She's still a bitch just not the one I made her out to be. Some people just don't ever get it, and Tasha was one of them. Like I tried to tell her before, you can't stop me and Edrick from being friends. It was too much for her to handle because shortly after that conversation we got right back into it. She's mad at me for something I have no control over. And the funny thing about it soon after that they broke up.

For good.

Edrick,

My love for you will never end and that's the problem. It needs to end and most of all needs to stop. But tell me how can you just stop feeling the way you once felt about someone? By me still loving you, and holding on to you makes me think that theirs hope for us and still something between us when there's nothing there. Some days I hate you, I hate the fact that I was head over heels for you. I hate the fact that I love you always had, always will and will continue too even though it seems that you don't love me. Most of all I hate the fact that I can't hate you even though I should. I used to love you but I can't love you anymore. I'm not your wifey anymore

and I refuse to be the bitch or hoe. If I have to be that I just shouldn't be in your in life anymore. It's just everything Tasha sees in you I saw it once upon a time. How she feels about you I felt it. The only thing about it is that what you see in her you can't see in me and how you feel about her you don't feel the same about me. I'm glad you getting your life on the straight and narrow or at least trying to and I always knew I'd see the day you'd get your GED.
Love Always Ericka.

        I can tell you first hand that no boy is worth all that confusion, No boy should ever break your heart. If Edrick really cared for me like he said none of this would have happened. I blame Taye Dunk forever introducing me, but at the same time it was a lesson learned. I didn't want to give up, I honestly thought that he would one day open his eyes. Maybe he's not the one who needs to open them. We started back talking and continuing the friendship that we knew was meant to last. I'm not gonna lie it feels great talking to Edrick. And yes sometimes I go back down memory lane but I keep those things to myself. He's my best friend and for anyone to think that I'll give that up they're stupid. I guess I hold on because if I remember then he won't forget.

    You'll Be Back Someday
No matter where you are, no matter who you're with
It doesn't even matter cuz I'll still be in this shit
No matter where you go, no matter what you say
It doesn't matter cuz you'll be back someday
I kept you in my prayers and tried to keep you in my heart
You said we'd be together even though were apart
So I sit by the window wasting, and rotting away
Looking out into the distance thinking you'll be back someday
No matter if your by yourself, or if your with someone new
It bothers me a little because I wonder can she do I what I can do
So before completely lose my mind all the way
To keep my sanity I laugh and tell them you'll be back someday
Hanging with my boys or chillen with the girls
I hear them whisper and say hateful words
They say you're in a relationship, I thought it wouldn't stay
So I tell them you'll be back someday
The first time I saw you with her I began to cry
I didn't think you loved her I thought I was a lie
I see you pass my direction so I turn and walk away

I mumble under my breath and mutter you'll be back someday
Whenever I get stuck and don't know what you say
I look up to the clouds and smile you'll be back someday
I used to think you'll be back, I used to think and only that. I hope your happy cuz I'm getting there now, don't know why don't really know how. You'll be back that ship has sailed, you'll be back that idea has failed. I stood by you and looked like a fool all because I thought it was cool. I see that you love her and don't love me. You locked my heart and won't give back the key. Now I'm moving on with my and I can say I don't care if you don't come back someday.

Some days I still have hope in my heart, I highly doubt that I'll ever give up or ever really give in. I find myself talking to him for hours and hours, he is the only boy that I ever even really trusted. I told him that I would always be there for him standing by his side when he wasn't even able to stand for himself or when nobody else would be there. Even though Edrick wasn't a good friend too me wasn't gonna make me become a bad friend. When he apologized for cheating on me, leaving me, and cheating with me made me ball like a fucking baby. It's like karma's a bitch and it hurts people who think they are incapable of getting hurt. To try to keep someone else from getting hurt and you get hurt is one hell of a feeling isn't it?

The thing about me and Edrick that Tasha and him ain't have was communication. He told me how he told her we weren't friends before we went out, that they weren't friends while they were going out, so what in the hell makes her think that they'll be friends after the fact. With us we were friends before we went out, we were the best or friends while we were going out and even though we aren't together now were still the friends and that friendship gets stronger and stronger everyday.

Dear Edrick,

First off please don't take these words your about to read the wrong way because as difficult as it is for you to read this is as difficult for me to write. But they need to be said. I need closure.

This will be the very last letter that you will ever going to get because it is the very last letter I am ever going to write. When it comes to you I can't make up my mind, I don't know what to do or say, how to act think or feel. One day I hate you and the next day I love you to death. I cry tears of confusion hurt and pain and then those tears are over taken by the smiles you've placed upon my face. Today I want to be with you and then tomorrow I don't. I make you out to be the bad guy thinking it will help me move on and its best we go our separate ways. Then I can't help but defend you and get defensive when anyone criticizes you. Telling them that deep down you are truly a good man

Over the years I've developed thick skin. I now know that crying does nothing it doesn't change what's going on though it gets it out of my system. I learned moving on is easier said then done. I can honestly say that you changed my life for the better and sometimes the worst. As the days goes by I never stopped caring. If I haven't left yet what makes you think I'd leave now? But I want to you to be happy even if it's not with me. I want to see you smiling even if I'm not the one who puts that smile on your face. What we have is unexplainable uncontrollable and unheard of but they have no clue.

Edrick I don't want to cry anymore. I have no tears left to cry anymore. And I know you don't wanna see me hurt you don't wanna make me cry anymore than what you already have don't you? One day you'll move on and I'll grow up and we'll look back thinking what if? I guess now we'll never know. Babe things happen for a reason, you were put in my life for a reason whatever that reason may be. People change so you can learn to let go, things fall out of order so others can fall into place. We'll find each other some day, one day I hope. I told you I forgave you a long time ago but now I fully forgive you, no more hard feelings.

I wonder are you ever gonna slow down and commit, or you were never ready or ever gonna commit to me. That's one hell of a feeling to wonder if the boy you love really loves you and nobody should have to feel that way. Nobody deserves it. So I guess this it the official ending of us. Sorry I had to end it in a letter but I don't have the balls to say it while you're listening. We need space, maybe a while when we stop calling. For that time I didn't hear from you at first I lost my mind then it came to pass. I cleared my mind and now it's at ease. My purpose isn't to hurt you or have you hate me but I had to tell you some way somehow. You aren't willing or even ready or it hasn't even crossed your mind about committing to me. You can't be my world if I am not the center of yours. Hellos are so much easier and goodbyes are so hard. After you say hello you catch feelings and always want them in your life and can't stand to see them walk away.

So with this letter I end it the same way I started it by saying this will be the very last letter that you will ever going to get because it is the very last letter I am ever going to write.

If you love someone they say let it go, but letting go is hard to do it's tough to swallow watching the one you love turn around and love someone else. Your too afraid that they wont come back, or that you'll be making the biggest mistake of your life. I learned that in life you have to take the risk. You're going to get heartbroken and dumped, you're going to be cheated on but when the signs are in your face don't ignore them. When you act as if it doesn't exist or bother you it's just gone keep happening. I will always love Edrick and nothing or on one will ever change that. We have our ups and downs but it makes our friendship be able to stand the test of times.

I just couldn't go through with letting go because he was my first love and meant everything to me. But giving up doesn't always mean you are weak; sometimes it means that you are strong enough to let go. And as I grow older I know there's a life after Edrick. I could wait and wait on something I thought was worth waiting for because of our past but I could be missing out on something new while I'm sitting here crying over what's old.

I always knew the day would come when you'd find somebody else, but in the back of my mind I couldn't picture you being with anyone else but me. I ask myself how did we make this far? Is it because we have so much in common? No its my ability to forgive and forget to act as if it never happened or it doesn't bother me. Losing you is not a risk that I'd ever be willing to take but as I get older and think about my future, I realize that I can't fault you for any of this. I understand your lonely I am too but I'm not going to just jump in some new relationship to feel satisfaction, to pass the time and get my mind off of you. Because that's not fair I can't just break anyone's heart and play with their emotions. I fell in love with a boy three years older than me because I was young and didn't know any better. But I still cant help but to be in love with a boy who deep down I know is never gonna work out between us. There is a love between us that no one can understand sometimes not even us. Time has never been on our side. But we always find our way back to one another. But one day when we go on our own paths, we'll walk and never look back

Everybody is quick to judge and speak their mind on Edrick's and my relationship. But they can shut the hell up because everybody has an Edrick. There first true love that they felt wasn't supposed to ever end. That relationship were you base everything on what was and not what it is now when it's right in front of your face.

You're so blind you're willing to settle for less because you think you love them. When you say you're over them but still tear up at the sight of their face. When you were happy and in love with the past you have no clue what's right in front of you now.

He told me that I'd never have to worry about anyone ever hurting me he was like "I got you, I'm like fingers and toes you can always count on me" but a lot change in just a matter of seconds or the moment a piece of pussy comes along, because even though I was the one who cared for Edrick I wasn't there and I knew he wanted me to touch, to smell, to feel, to love and hold. Edrick, the one who said I could always count on him the one who said he'd never hurt me again, became undependable and hurt me once again but this time was worse because deep down I knew better and I believed him. Edrick, the man who said he'd never break another promise broke them once again. Edrick, the man who was so loving and warm was so bitter and cold. Edrick, the one who said he'd never leave made like a banana and split, taking my heart with him now I'm one cold heartless emotionless bitch. Edrick, the man who I'd give the world to and die for shot me in the heart and felt no remorse

It hurt me so bad but deep down I knew it was for the best.

I stood before him feeling as if I was looking at a complete stranger, because the man in front of me was not the same man I feel in love with years ago. Nothing he could say could fix the damage he caused. Tears began to roll down my face, because I was in such disbelief that this is what we had become. The love I thought could stand the test of time couldn't even survive 4 years. But deep down I felt as if it was my fault because I allowed it to go on. He grabbed my face and whispered.

There are something's that are meant holding on too, and yet there are something's we have to let go. There are some questions that we always find the answers too, but some answers we'll never know. There are some moments you wish you could do over, and some moments you'd never take back. There are some roads that keep you focused, and some that throw you off track.There are some people you'd wish you'd forget and those who are close to your heart. There are friends who stray away in distance and those where nothing can tear you apart

There are faces that blend in with the crowd, and faces that will never fade away There are some days you have all the right words to brighten someone's day

There are some words better left unsaid, however some that need to be spoken

There are some door that are meant to be closed, and some that are better open.

There are some things that better us and some things that are better off

I'm so glad I met you, because you changed my life, and he changed mine as well. We were young and now we have our whole life to figure out what it is that we want. But this isn't what I want? I never asked to meet you, let alone feel the way I feel about you, but things happen and feelings that were once so strong become weak. but It's things like this that are better off. Your better off single, not having to cry, worrying about me, loving someone who loves you but not the same way you do.

He kissed my lips and said goodbye and before I got the chance to say I forgive you or goodbye. I realized it was all just a dream.

Zoë

Sometimes what you want isn't always what you need

You know you when you have someone who gets your attention, and you want them to stay in your eyesight. That's how it was with Zoe, when I saw him I was mind boggled. The first time I saw Zoe I wanted to get him and keep him. He stood out the crowd, he was the cutest face I'd ever seen at Webber. Just so I could see him I walked down that hallway and had it down like clockwork so it always worked in my favor. A year had passed and I walked down a new hallway to see plenty new faces, still hoping to see that old face in that old hallway. September 28th there was something about that day something wouldn't let me go the direction I was headed. So I walked down that old hallway and there he was. By the time I got the balls to speak to him he was gone. I felt so stupid if I only spoke, will I speak next time if there will ever be another?

I blew my chance to speak again, what the hell was the matter with me? When I got close to him my throat got all dry and even if I could speak what would I say? It wasn't like I say yeah boy I been watching you for about a year now. I dint want to seem like I was crazy or a stalker before I even got to know him. I was determined to get that boy anyway possible. I wasn't worried about being pressed or looking stupid because when I want something I get it. So I swallowed my pride and stopped being such a cry baby and spoke to the damn boy. At first I chocked and began to sweat but it was now or never. I'm guessing he liked the fact I spoke to him, because soon after that me and Zoe went out. By Zoe being a seventh grader and I being an eighth grader didn't matter but it did bother me a bit. As long I got to see and be with Zoe's made up for that the first time Zoe told me he loved me I hesitated to say it back. I was afraid to love Zoe, I was afraid to open up and let him in. I didn't know if I could trust him due to Edrick but everyone's different. I wanted Zoe and me to have this bond that could never be broken. I was merely terrified that if I fell was he going to catch me?

I told Zoe that I wanted more for us. He simply said what you want isn't always what you need. I hated that we were so honest, there was no lying in our relationship. I don't think that honesty is always the best policy there's just something's I didn't think I could handle to know. I wanted him to be truthful so we didn't have to be in an unhappy and untruthful relationship. Zoe had asked me how I would have felt if he had more than one girlfriend. I thought he was joking he couldn't be for real. Again I rather him break up with me than continue a relationship that wasn't going to work. I told Zoe do whatever he wanted because no matter what I said or how I felt he was going to do what he wanted. I felt telling him that was a mistake I had to learn. If I hadn't let him just run free he'd still be mine completely.

It was hard seeing Zoe in the hallway, that exact same hallway where I first laid eyes n him. Why did I still go down that hall anymore anyway? There was just something about that place that I wanted to remember. I felt by not going down that hallway I was running away from what was. I told those girls whenever they said *"isn't that your man"* that he was just a puppy off his lease that wasn't ready to come back home. After he's done playing games he'll be home where he belongs. Though that little puppy never made it back home, he wandered and wasn't coming back. I remained his friend though even after I left High School never asking him what went wrong because I didn't care to know. Though there are times when I beat myself up and blame myself. I should have fought a little bit harder and tried just a little bit more.

Moving on is hard to do even when you know it's true. There's nothing else, there's nothing left. You gave it your all you gave it your best. Why was I still stuck on the past? I guess because that's when I felt safe and if I knew this is what we would have become I wouldn't have let it go on any further.

In January it's cold and snowy but today was nice and somewhat warm because the sun was out. So I called Zoe and said we should spend some time together and get a lot of things out the way. When I opened the door I didn't recognize the boy that was standing in front of me. That cute boy had matured out of that face. But he still had his charm and gotten way better at his game and I became one of those girls Zoe told me about. I felt so dumb and stupid I ruined the friendship that I tried so desperately to keep. I was never able to look at him the same.

My sister Meech's birthday and we were all having a good time but good things don't last forever. My smile went sour when I was introduced to Zoe's girlfriend. I couldn't believe I was faced to face with the girl he was trying to settle things down with. I couldn't help but suspect did she know? Was I giving off this vibe or strange energy? Or was I just really trippin? I felt like the pink elephant in the room. It was awkward only because I was letting it I wasn't about to ruin my night. So I just stopped caring.

Then Zoe walked in and was in disbelief that not only were we holding a conversation but laughing and having a good time. We said hello and that was pretty much it. Whenever Zoe looked my direction I was already looking in his. After they all went to bed I laid up and started thinking. I didn't want to come between them due to my indiscretion and Zoe's infidelity. One night, that wasn't supposed to happen the way it did, not under those conditions.

Zoe never took me serious and that was the problem. I was just his friend and only that, mind you I was ok with it but he acted as if we weren't ever anything more. I learned to understand it and respect that. Zoe was just a boy and I was just a girl, we were just two kids who looked for something different in each other.

The one thing that Zoe and I had was good times and lots of laughter. There was never a time when I wasn't enjoying myself around him. Things come and go but the lessons you learn will always last a lifetime. It means more than any break up and more than any friendship. It's something that I can never get back and now that I see where we are now I can leave it as is. I never got until now what Zoe meant by what you want isn't always what you need. Though I wanted us to work we needed space and plus, I knew we were better off as friends. We had so much fun laughing and talking. And not once have I ever looked back because Zoe leaving me was an eye opener for me.

A friend of mine, and I were thinking, what would the world had been like if the world was perfect, and you were still with the very first person you fell in love with? Could you image what your life would be like? Can you visualize yourself happy? And if you are a parent could you image if you had kids by someone else, do you think them and your new kids would have any similarities. Being a parent is the best joy in the world, just think having new kids, new names, new personalities? If life was anything like that I would still be with Zoe. Now I'm ashamed to say that he was my first real boyfriend, way back when I was in the 7th grade. And to think of where we were and where we are now makes me a little sad. We don't even speak; I can barely get a reply text back from him. Can I see where we'd be now? Sometimes I can, I can see us too crazy ass people with young, wild, and free personalities, sitting back laughing smoking a blunt, and sipping on drank. I could see us getting tattoos all the time. As much as I could image this, I know it isn't true, it just wasn't us.

Scooter
At some point you stop living in the moment

There was once a love between us two, a love once shared with me and you. I don't know where it went all I can say it was time well spent. I don't know what it was and what happened but it was a learning experience. You ever had someone that everyone said was no good? Deep down you knew it was true but didn't want to miss out on something better yet someone you've never had. You can't always judge a book by its cover so you skim through the pages to see if it's any good. It's a waste of time to read a book you're not interested in but you are passionate about finishing what you started.

I saw him when the first time when I came back from New Jersey. I had begged my momma to let me go to SVRC because I wasn't doing anything by staying in the house for the remainder of the summer. There were things I had to do and people I needed to see. Plus, it would be good to get my mind right and get the feel of going to school again before September arrived. I walked in the building and immediately my eyes were on the two boys I had not seen last school year.

Since Dale had left me and went to the Hill Scooter and I had gotten a little closer. It wasn't me being rude but I couldn't see me and Scooter going any further. I went to his house and sat on his front step and that was the moment he started to grow on me. He was so foolish and that's what caught my attention. The first time he kissed me it felt wrong but then again oh so right. It would be special if I let it and all I had to do was give in. But giving in meant giving up on Dale and I wasn't ready to do that just yet. But loneliness took over and Scooter was always there. I liked it when he took control, the way he grabbed me and pulled me towards him. The way he grabbed my breasts, and sucked my neck. The way he looked down at me when he was on top of me, and how the sweat dripped off of him and on to me, and when we were done he would just lay there, how I could not only hear his breaths, but feel them. I loved that I could just lay on him. No matter who was in the house, or where we were that never stopped us.

Scooter: "Oh my God bae, I love you and I ain't going nowhere"

Ericka; "Scooter babe I love you too, and promise you that you not gone leave"

Scooter; "Ericka I ain't gone leave you imma stay as long as you want me too"

Now where have I heard that before, and that made me grow afraid. I wanted to believe Scooter but only time would tell but I wasn't ready to wait, I wasn't going to let Scooter break my heart. What I loved about us was that we never faked anything, how Scooter and I still went on with our day. We didn't base our relationship on forever we just lived for the moment whatever happened just going to happen, I just went with the flow. Some people took us as a joke then others looked as if we really were trying to be something. I feel like this, you shouldn't have to make someone promise that they won't leave, they should want to stay on their own.

Mrs. Antra: "I'm not trying to be all in your business but I hope you're not rushing into things with Scooter just to prove a point or just to get over the fact Dale's gone. You and Scooter are a very odd couple."

I respected Mrs. Antra's opinion although it went in one ear and out the other. I wasn't about to stop the way I was feeling. Why is it you always have that one person sticking their noise where it doesn't belong? Maybe it's because they care and are looking out for you or are just noisy ass people. Even though she was looking out for me I didn't want to hear what she had to say. I spent too much time listening to what other people had to say on what was my relationships, even though what they were saying was good advice, it was still advice I wasn't trying to hear. I spent a lot of time with Scooter in hopes to get over Dale and I fell faster and harder than I ever thought possible. Nobody understood that even though he was an ass hole he had a compassionate side and a loving and caring side.

For the longest time I along with a whole bunch of other chicks would chill at the house but slip out the back door as they momma got home. I was horrified to meet her because she was always yelling. Once three-thirty came around we was out that house scattering like cockroaches. I got sick of sneaking out, only hood rats and hoes who were girlfriend material went out the back door. I wanted to be able to leave out the same door I came in. I wanted his mom not only just to know who I was but like me also.

I was sitting on the coach in between Scooter's legs when we heard her pull up. Scooter looked at me as if I was supposed to have gotten up and ran, I wasn't for it anymore. I sat there and when it was time for me to speak I didn't get tongue tied or anything, she simply waved and went in the room. Meeting someone's mom

Sweetest day was coming and I had to get my babe something. This was the first holiday I ever spent with somebody, so it had to be special. Being that he was from the Southside whatever I got him had to be yellow. I searched and sought but couldn't find anything until the last minute. I got him a yellow due rag a big red and yellow balloon and a card that read.

I know it hasn't been long but it's been a long time coming. The time we've shared I'll cherish and always remember forever but I do have to ask you. Are you fine with just living in the moment or can you see us moving a couple steps ahead? I feel blinded whenever I'm around you but as long as you lead me in the right direction I'll be fine.

When Scooter walked me home I felt like the luckiest girl in the world.

Ericka: "Scooter what would you say if I told you I was pregnant? Would you still love me? Would you leave or stay? Would you want me too keep it, and most of all would you still love me no matter my choice?"

Scooter: "Bae we gone figure this out it's gone be tough but I'm here for you."

I felt this chill come over me and I hugged Scooter as tight as I could. This was real, this was us and I couldn't believe this was happening. He told me he was fine living in the moment because each moment was a step further. But there comes a time when you forget about that moment and start thinking about tomorrow and the next day or down the line. To reassure me that we'd be living in each moment he gave me his hoody. Shit he better had it was cold that day.

That hoody meant a lot to Scooter so it meant a lot to me, since it meant the world to him it meant the world to me. You couldn't get me to take it off it was my jacket and most of the time just my shirt. I felt like Scooter was always with me. I didn't care if he wasn't the smartest kid in the class not all of us are straight A student's. When you care for someone you stop thinking of just yourself. At that point Scooter stopped being selfish, he realized that in order to get love he had to give it. Then comes a time when you stop living in the moment and start living for the future.

Mind you nobody's perfect, there was days when I just wanted to walk out that door. I wouldn't just be walking out on us, I couldn't look at myself in the same light if I left. Was my own insecurity worth losing the boy that I gave up so much for? I'd be walking out on myself giving up when I knew that I shouldn't. I wanted to leave before I got hurt because I was scared and didn't know which way was right. I'd be walking out on a promise, a promise that wasn't even in stone, but still a promise I wasn't ready to break.

We were young, we were stupid and most of all we were caught up in the moment. I couldn't help but think what things would have been like but I was better off not thinking about it or ever bringing it back up. I don't know if things would have been a mistake, or if they could have had potential to be much more than Scooter and I? That was my secret that I would take to the grave.

I learned what it means to over stay your welcome. I

was with him every single day looking at the same faces. I was young and to me there was no need to see the same faces day after day, day in and day out. Things started to spiral out of control with me and Scooter. I couldn't stand the sight of him at times because he was a flirt and would flirt with other people right in front of my face. Then there were times when I couldn't even look him in the eye because I felt guilty. So I became distant then there were days I wanted him to just hug me. He stopped calling me bae and started calling me a bitch or rachette. When you become that bitch you become nothing. You mean nothing to him. You get no attention because he got what he wanted. To me a bitch is the worst thing a boy can call you because that lets you know he don't respect you.

I still tried and did it with a smile on my face in order to hide the tears. I didn't want everyone all up in my business saying they told me so. I was pretending to be happy but why? I don't know but I learned that not even the biggest smile can fake or cover up the truth. I felt like shit, like nothing what was I doing settling for less? Because that less was once something much more. Me and Scooter got into it that night so I left, and Stacy stayed. What pissed me off the most was that Stacy allowed them to talk trash about me. You say you told them to stop but since they didn't you remained there and let them.

I couldn't hold on to that hoody anymore. It held to many memories, too many painful memories that needed to be let go. I don't know why I felt bad it wasn't as if Scooter promised me anything. I walked in the classroom and cut that hoody into as many pieces as possible. Every piece was a piece of my heart being ripped out of my chest. I poured glue on top of it and placed it on his seat with a letter. This bullshit meant the world to me because it meant everything to you. I cherished it and valued it more than you ever have done for me. Even if you try and glue the pieces back like our relationship it will never be the same. I don't know if I should hate you or feel sorry for you. Sorry that you can't see what's right in front of your face.

I would still walk up and down that street, and glance at the house like I did when I first met him. The only thing different was that my smile was never shown again. I couldn't even hold my head up, my head hung down and the only time I stopped was when someone called my name. Still I would ask about Scooter how he was doing and how he had been. One day I was walking past and actually didn't even pay the house no attention. I heard this yell looked back and kept on walking. This car rolled up on the side of me and it was Marty.

Marty: "Damn girl you looked like a bad bitch from the back."

So what did I look like from the front? It paid me no never mind because I knew I gained niggas attention. I don't know why but I saw myself starting to like Marty. I laughed and flirted a lot. I could have had sex with Marty at any given time I wanted too but I didn't because Scooter didn't deserve it. I found myself having a crush on Marty but I knew it wasn't right and I tried my hardest to fight it. He was like a brother too me, I would always go to him for advice, we could laugh and talk and joke around. I did something so stupid, how was it that I found myself in the comforts of his brother Marty? This is the reason why you drink, I mean I was pissy drunk, and my true feelings came out that night. I felt numb, I barely remember anything, all I knew was that what I did was wrong, a part of me cared thinking to myself, damn I'm no better than these other lil bitches that come up and through here. But I thought, one night couldn't hurt as long as it never got out it would be our little secrets but there are no such things as secrets in the Harris house.

It seemed as if those hood rats still had come and gone, still creeping out the back door like the hoes they were meant to be. I was still the only one who could walk in and out the same door anytime I pleased. Scooter momma and I had gotten real close. I would still come around because his family grew on me. I loved everyone in his family. Marty, Jamie, Keisha, Kie, Quanie, Diamond and Jas all had a place in my heart. Even with all that went on Scooter still had a place in my heart. Every moment you spend with someone they tend to grow on you, planned or unplanned, you gain feelings you never knew you had or could feel about someone when you weren't supposed to have them in the first place.

Scooter ran in the house with blood dripping down his lip. I couldn't stand the sight of seeing him in pain. So we had to take him to the emergency room, and who was there wasn't any of the chicks he was calling wifey but I was. Who else besides me had Scooter's best interest at heart? We waited about two hours before they even looked at him. I didn't even think what my mom would do if she came home and I wasn't there. I would have just had to get in trouble, because some things are more important than punishment. Scooter knew I loved him and that's why he treated me that way because he knew I didn't want to leave. I'm so disappointed that it got this way when it wasn't really supposed to be nothing at all. I guess what you want isn't always what you need.

Time Well Spent

You had me writing you letters left and right, you were all I thought about at night. Looking back at our first kiss that's something I dearly miss. I'll never forget because that time was time well spent. We showed our love in our own kinda way, looked at each other for hours with nothing to say. You hugged me so tightly, so tightly and true and from that moment on I thought it was you. I miss those days but those days were time well spent. A love once shared between us two, a love once shared with me and you. I don't know where it went all I can say it was time well spent.

I wrote this letter a million times and it still never seems right. You bought my favorite now or laters and that tells me you cared because you remembered. I don't deserve anybody who can sit here and call me no bitch. The difference between that Ericka and this Ericka today is that bitch stayed and tolerated yo bullshit and this bitch is walking away.

What Scooter means to me now is like what a penny is compared to a dollar. Worthless, but I keep those pennies, in my back pocket, because they come in handy every now and again.

It was getting rather late and my ride was nowhere to be found, I had dozed off to sleep and when I woke up it was past midnight. I didn't feel right asking to stay and spend the night but I had no other choice. She didn't even trip and let me go back to sleep. I slept in the bed with Scooter, it made me think back on how we were back in September. I stared at him just wondering what went wrong and how he could lie there asleep as if nothing was going on. How could he just lay there as if I didn't even exist? How could I lie next to him after what he had done? Worst how could I lie there after what I had done, blocking it out as if it never happened?

Dale

When you're nothing more than a bet there's nothing more to expectThat high some people get when they cut themselves is high I get when Dale's name comes to mind. I still to this day get a rush that never fades away. He's the drug I think I'll always be addicted too. From the moment I met him he stole my heart, and it didn't bother me at all because even though things were rough he held on and hasn't let go. I'll forgive him no matter what he does, no matter how stupid and ignorant he is because he's human. I think I was most attracted to him because I knew he wasn't mine. And when we were together, it was just simple, it was easy.

Like I said my attention went back and forth from Dale to Scooter. The time I didn't spend playing with Scooter I was being serious wit Dale. I was confused and didn't know who to choose. Dale and I had this up close and personal connection, with the way we cut our eyes and knew what we were thinking without saying a word. I was walking with Pooh Pooh down the hallway when Dale grabbed me and said he couldn't be talking to his girl. Last time I checked I wasn't nobody chick but I liked the fact he was into me.

Ericka: "Look Dale I like you and I want you to be honest with me. If you got something to say just say it, don't hold back or sugar coat nothing. I had been hurt to many times before I aint trying to face rejection no time soon. I'm tired of making a complete ass of myself."

I have a tendency of speaking things to soon. Right after my feelings started to mature Dale left and went to the Hill. I didn't want him to leave because I wanted us to work. For the first time I didn't have to think on how I felt with him I didn't have to try. I thought this was all too good to be true in the first place.

Dale: "I aint gone lie to you, it's gone be hard. I'm not gone say I won't talk to any other girls but I'll hold on to you."

I thought what happens when somebody fills my spot? He started talken to this girl name Passion who I used to be cool with but couldn't stand anymore. We were going through the toughest challenge ever called distance. The minutes felt like hours and the hours felt like days that we were apart. All that loneliness needed to be filled and that's when Scooter came into place. So I had to tell him about how I started to care for Scooter, weeks had passed and I couldn't hold it any longer.

Ericka: "Babe it was never my intent to hurt you, lead you on or make you think that I was playen you. The truth of it all is that you have a girl and I have a man and there's nothing we can do about it. What else can I say things happen"

Truly I felt bad it was hard for those words to even leave my lips, but the truth is we aren't together and there is nothing between us more than lust. We were living our own lives and kept combining the two. What was I supposed to do wait for Dale to leave Passion? I found comfort in Scooter and wasn't going to lie about it. It was unexpected and happened way to fast. It wasn't like I was trying to play either one, I just fell for them both. Things happen only because we let them happen, things happen because we sometimes have the choice to let them happen or not.

Dale: "Since we being all honest, I guess now would be the best of the worst times to tell you this. You were nothing more than a bet."

Nothing more than a bet, and all this time I was worried about hurting this boy feelings. Damn those little bastards they knew what they were doing all along when I was over here contemplating on who I would talk too. Tears rolled down my faced I swallowed my tongue and just hung up. I was heart broken and didn't know how to feel, so I called back to hear his reasoning's. I felt so stupid to get caught up in mixed emotions and let them get the best of me. All this time I was worried about hurting one if not both when they didn't give a damn about me.

Ericka: "Wow and to think I was the one who felt bad I should have played you cuz you were playen me from jump."

Dale: "It ain't even like that. I felt bad and I started to care about you, I love you."

Ericka: "No Dale you don't love me, when you love someone you don't lie or beat around the bush. Remember it was just a bet nothing less but I guess you tried to make it more. You can't have your cake and eat it too."

But wasn't it I who was doing the same? By going back and forth between him and Scooter, but I think the only difference was, were our intentions. I never intended for things to get this deep to go this far, and honestly neither did Dale. But does anybody ever mean for a situation to go oh so far. And when people's feelings are involved that's what hurts even more, because when you start to care for someone, when you share things with people, let them into your most intimate moments, when you talk to them about any and everything you start to feel something for them. Something that when it gets taken away, or you thought more of it then they did, you feel stupid, you feel hurt and most of all you feel broken, but when you were once broken before and started putting the pieces back together it makes you just want to throw that old heart away. Throwing away any and everything you ever felt and you just want to start over, with no feelings no emotions, and no old memories. You don't ever want to remember any heartache or heartbreak. You just want to be whole and complete, but it's never that's simple is it?

Why do I even try? I think we just need to let go and say goodbye. You make me feel worthless and now I'm starting to think you did it on purpose. Tell me why should I hold on when you're giving up. You're committing love suicide. -Ester Dean

Sitting there killing me softly.

Dale

I never thought once would I ever doubt the feelings I have for you. I understand what you and Passion have but what about us and what we had? Are you willing to throw all of that away because I'm gone or just because you're scared? Well I'm scared too but I won't let my fear hold me back from getting the love I so truly deserve. I hate the fact I was a bet gone wrong. As of right now I understand I'll never be Passion I'll never be your girlfriend. But you and I both know I should be. But what do you expect me to do? Sit here like a dummy and wait for you when we both know you're not going to leave her.

You're like an adrenaline rush and I love that feeling but it's starting to make me sick. I still want you by side we were like Bonnie and Clyde in love and ready to ride. I'm serious when I say once I'm gone I'm not coming back. The old Ericka would have stayed like the dumb bitch she was, but I'm not that dumb bitch anymore. So what's it gonna be? I can't make up your mind for you Dale, I want you to see in me what I see in you.

Just because I said I care for you doesn't mean I'll let you play me for a sucka. I realized what the problem was between us, we aren't committed to one another and will never be committed. How is it I love you and you love me when I have Scooter and you have Passion. "Secret lovers is what we are, try so hard to deny the way we feel, but we both belong to someone else and we can't let it go." We both know that we aren't being faithful and at first I was fine with that and you may be fine with that but I can't settle for that anymore.

It's insane that you have such a negative hold on me and I can't let go, because I like it. Is it insane that I want what I can't have? That I can reach you but can't grasp you. It's insane that you're not mine and it makes me want you more and I'll do whatever it takes too keep you. Is it insane that I'm hooked on a feeling and it's got me so high up I have no clue what it's like to come down? It's insane that I love you and I know you don't feel the exact same way I do.

I can't be trying to make all kind of arrangements when I got Scooter and you can't be lying to Passion bout who you with. So we need to just let it go and call it quits before anyone else gets hurt, too attached and before we refuse to let go.

Quason

Quason is just an unsolved puzzle, it's just no other way to put it. Even if I put all the pieces together, I have no idea what it is that I'm supposed to be seeing. It's funny because the day I met him wasn't even planned. Instead of me going the direction I normally go I just walked down Cherry. I heard an "Aye Girl" somewhere far in the distance walked his way, now that's that let me holla shawty shit I was talking about before. Now normally I wouldn't have even stopped for some bullshit ass attention getter like that. After school I would go over on twelfth and just chill with him. Whenever I get around him I act like a kid in the candy store, my maturity level just drops drastically. I can't help but giggle and smile.

Now, I know I was moving a little fast with him but I got tired of standing still. When I moved back with my dad I was mad because I really was feeling this boy. It was hard but we tried, right before I went to bed he would be the last phone call I'd make. I wanted his voice to be the last voice I heard before I went to sleep. I told that whatever he needed, I got him if I had it he would too. He told me that no girl ever loved him enough to send him money, and I simply told him I'm not like other girls.

When Quason told me he missed me it really meant a lot to hear that. It made me feel special because I had been questioning it, if I was just some face in the crowd or the one he'd remember. It wasn't like I wanted Quason to love me all I wanted was to know that he cared that I meant something to him as he did too me. I never thought that we'd be were where at because distance is the hardest thing to overcome. Why do I even put up with his bullshit sometimes? Because he's worth it I think?

I never questioned myself as much as I do when it comes down to you. I like you really I do but it makes me wonder how much you truly like me. I can't have a nigga who can't take the time to call me or even not answer the phone when I call. Now I hate ever meeting you cause if I never would have never met you none of these feelings would be here right now. I feel so stupid but no regrets just lessons learned. It's like everybody knows the way I feel about you except you.

I think with this boy I bit off a little more than I could chew. Just because something taste good doesn't mean you should stuff your face in it. Deon warned me not to get involved and being the hard headed girl I am I didn't listen. Now I'm in too deep. I'm just so confused and if I could ask Quason anything is if he really means it? If he says yes I wanna see how he says it I wanna hear some type of passion in his voice to let me know he's for real, I wanna see the look in his eye when he tells me. I don't want Deon to be right and then I don't want Quason to be wrong.

The one thing I hate about Quason is that he doesn't understand that I care not just for him but about him. I want him to see where I'm coming from I want him to call me and see what it's like to not answer the phone or hang up in his face. People tell me leave him alone he's no good, but do I listen? Hell no! So for a while I did the unthinkable and stopped calling him. Every day I ask myself why am I holding on to this boy in the first place? Why don't I just let him go while it's early so I don't fall so hard and become afraid to get up? I hold on to him because deep down I believe there's a chance, I want to believe there's hope. When someone means this much to you they must be important. I just know he'll come around one day, but when is that day. Will I do what's good for me and just say were better off as friends?

Quason

I never had the courage to tell you how I was feeling and I feel as if I have to tell you before it's too late. I like you and I see myself falling for you and I don't know why? I ask myself every day what is it about you that keeps me, Well I keep telling myself that there will always be a one day, but neither one of us can sit around and wait for that one day if we know one day will never get here. You'll find a girl and I'll have a man and we'll go our separate ways. Keep watch over your little sister cuz I love the hell outta Tati, I really grew close to her over these last couple months. Most of all stay safe.

I knew the kind of nigga Quason was. That hood ass no good nigga that ya momma warned you about and the boy you father tries to keep you away from, but the more they keep you away from the closer you go. I take full responsibility, in whatever happens between us, because I let it happen, I let myself fall too fast, too hard, over what? Niggas talk real good game, but when is it that a nigga stops being a nigga and starts to become a man? When is it that he puts his gang banging days aside and settles down? Is it possible to love someone like Quason, who has girls at his feet, got bitches for days, weeks, hell a lifetime?

Sometimes I wonder without your hood lifestyle how many bitches would you have falling at your feet. Without your background who the fuck are you tell me that? If it wasn't for the things you do I would have never even heard about you, and hell maybe without my background you would have never known about me either? What was it about me that got your attention? Because the first time you met me you just randomly stopped me, what if I wasn't pretty? What if I didn't turn out to be so sweet and loving like I am now? What if I never gave you the fucking time of day? Would you have still chased, or just went on to the next. Was I an easy target? The guns don't make the man, so without it who and what are you? What is it that you stand for?

So many questions run through my mind that I want you to answer, but the one thing of all that I really wanna know was any of this real? Was it just my imagination running away with me? Was there some point in time when any of this meant something to you or were you just running game and fuckin with my head? What is it that I ever did too you? What did I do to deserve getting played? I was there when you needed someone, I was your bank, your personal atm, and all because I thought I was proving a point to show you that I cared. I wanted to show you that I got you, whatever you need what's mine is yours, but never again, I worked for mines, and I'll be damned if I give a nigga what I worked for and not even the simplest thank you. What kind of girl do you really think I am? Because I know your kind, and I always find myself falling for your type, you might be a man legally, but in every aspect you're still a boy. Got your priorities all fucked up, life isn't about how many hoes you got, or the hood you with, sadly your just another nigga who fell victim of the streets of Saginaw. -I need a strong, yet sensitive black man.....What kinda man is that?? -A man who got his shit together..

He got his own can take care of him self and will still look out for me.. A man and not a nigga. One who knows where he comes from an never forgets it... One who can trust me an kno wifey got his back

Well I got my own i neva fagot were i came from i dam showl take care of myself and im 2 real-hahaha thats what i like too hear..seems like u got cha mind right tooo..

U kno it what kinda girl is u E -Im the kind of girl that is sweet an loving but don't tolerate bullshit...I mite not be the badest thing walken but I gotta inner beauty... I'm smart an got alot goin for myself.. I got big dreams and plan on makin them a reality..Imma hard ass workin girl

Sound str8 to me u might get sumthin gud u stay that way

-Thank you i hope so too. and dont u change cuz you'll get a girl Like me one day lol.. Hopefull one will fall right into my hands-yup.. same here... its like i been lookin fa mr right but settled for any and everything less. I'm glad we had this lil covo, its nice talking to someone real for once any time.u shoulda been fukin wit me. It's so strange because right after that I called him and we talked on the phone till about 4:30 that morning, just talking about life, and who we are and the things we liked. People called me corny they said "You taking it way back to the old days" I guess I'm just old school then because my parents taught me to get to know someone before you just jump into a relationship. Its ass backwards to say "Aww he fine, let's be a couple" and then you get to know them. What happens if once you get together you see how much of an ass he is or that you really don't even like him? I think people have their priorities in the wrong place.

How could something this right feel so wrong? It had me feeling like this is too good to be true. I forgot that Tarun's Quason right hand man, and we all know how there are rules on how you don't date someone you liked or smashes best friend, but you can't help who you like, you can't help who you feel feelings for. So this became my downfall and I was scared that if he found out he would look at me differently or wouldn't feel the same way towards me and we'd finish what we had before we even got started.

I didn't want to be one of those girls who talk to friends but that's not me. Alex and Emoni both told me you can't help who you like and that was just it. I couldn't help it, it just happened and I didn't want any bad feelings. So I told him that I had a secret, and he said in his cute voice "what is it?" I used to talk too well mess with someone that you really close wit.

No Privacy

"Who Quason?""Yea how'd you know" "I been knew that from
the day when I saw you on 12th" "Oh, well I just thought I'd throw
that out there but I never wanted to say nothing about it" "Why you
thought I wouldn't like you, look at you differently and say we can't
talk now"

     Right then at that moment I knew he was the one. Now
when I mean the one I mean the one boy who stands out. The one
who doesn't care about my past, what I did and who I been with.
He's the one who makes me feel special, the one who makes me
believe that true love is out there. People come into your life and
change it someway, somehow, they change the way you look at life,
the way you think, how you act and the way you feel.

     I couldn't help but think, if I could tell Tarun, why I
couldn't tell Quason? Wasn't he the one who needed to know? But I
didn't even know myself how to answer that question because even
though Quason and I have our moments, deep down he has a good
heart and though he has a funny way of showing it I know he cares.
And I couldn't hold that burden over my head, because Quason
didn't deserve to be lied to or played. I didn't think I was playing
him because I told him about Tarun but not as much as I should
have. I remember telling Quason once I care about you really I do
and whatever the outcome of all of this is I don't want you to be mad
at me or hate me. He told me he could never hate me and he really
does care for me and that I'm not losing him, but it's not him I'm
afraid of losing.

     Tarun came and saved me showing me what a real man
is supposed to be like. He changed my mind when I said every boy is
the same. He makes me laugh and I trust him. He's my future
boyfriend. I know it's kind of early to say I love him but I do. It's a
different type of love. It's a love that I never felt, a love I didn't have
to rush to feel, a love that gets stronger everyday, a love that I know
won't go away, a love that goes deeper beyond the word because
he's actions show it. Most of all it's a love that I don't have to
sugarcoat and pretend, I can be myself, and have no second guesses
about.

     Tarun and I talk about how girls liked him just because
of the life he lived and the fact he had more than a couple hundred
dollars in his pocket. I explained to him that ok that's cool and all but
who cares. I heard a lot about Tarun but getting with a dude for his
money wasn't my style. I didn't need a man to do for me when I
could do them for myself. I wasn't a gold digger. I like Tarun for his

personality, for the fact that we talked till the early morning. That there were no secrets, I liked calling him my future boyfriend. I loved stayed up until 5am laughing, giggling, and getting to know someone the way I wanted too. I felt comfortable, for the first time I felt safe.

No matter how far I go my past seems to catch up with me, and not only follow me but haunt me. I never been able to get why do people get mad when other people are happy? Why must be ruin a good thing? I'm not proud of my past, but is not me anymore, so why must people bring it up? Since I've moved I've heard plenty of reasons why I left. I was in rehab, but I didn't need rehab in order to seek recovery. And I got a baby too, but apparently I must not be a good mother cuz I had no clue.

Someone told Tarun about an old fling, saying I had sex with Joc and Jr which whoever told the story was way off track. Why even spread a story without having all the facts? For the first time I truly felt ashamed. For Tarun someone who didn't know anything about my past too be told such a thing that would make anyone second guess and look at you differently.

One thing I hate more than anything is when I expect too much of things. Now mind you I really like Tarun yeah I do but he stays so far away. Even though he told me I was going to be his future girlfriend what about now? One thing that hurts more than anything is when you aren't told about something and have to find it out on your own. I don't know if Tarun was just trying not to hurt my feelings and was looking out for me but the way it came to light was as if he was trying to hide something, and I hate secrets. I felt we were close enough to tell each other anything, whether it would hurt us or not. It's better to know the truth and accept it rather than to live in something of our own mind.

Tarun had been talking to this girl name Kooda, round the same time as me. The only reason how and why I found out about it was because she was writing me on Facebook telling me to leave her man alone, and that he was taken. So that didn't look too good in my eyes, because this random ass girl came out of nowhere. She had been stalking me for months, writing me telling me never to come back to Michigan, then she got my number, Lord only knows how? The one thing that kept running through my mind was that he had to be having sex with her. Because no girl is gonna act the way she does, play on my phone and constantly write me if she's not under the impression that he's her man.

So I had to ask him, even though I don't think I wanted to know but was he fucking her? He said yea, once or twice. I wanted him to tell me from jump because it's not like I could do anything about it. It's hard to accept the truth when it was kept from you all this time. It hurts deep down to know better, you think wow this is too good to be true and that's exactly what it was, too good to be true. I tell myself I have nothing to worry about but deep down I have a lot too. I don't live in Saginaw, nor do I or can I see Tarun. He might talk to me every single night, but he spends time with her. I'll never fully out know the truth.

Kooda tells me her and Tarun been talking for about two years and Tarun says more like two months. She says its love and he says it's nothing like that. As of this moment I could careless, what's done is done and there's nothing I could do about it. No matter how upset I was, no matter how mad, disappointed and angry I was that's what it was.

One thing I hate more than liars is drama. I can't handle it so I try not to surround myself in it. I hate girls who claim to be grown and are so fucking childish. Who prank call you breathing on the phone and harass you, honestly she shouldn't have the problem with me I feel as if she need to confront Tarun. Though I hate being petty, I told her I can't wait to go back to Michigan so I can fuck your so called man. It felt wrong but seeing her pissed made it all worth it.

I just wanna tell Kooda that I think she's childish and very petty. And if it's Tarun you want you can have him, but the question is does he really want because if it was love like she claimed, he wouldn't be denying her, to a girl who stays miles away, let alone any other female.

We had always been so honest with one another, so why start being secretive now? Why couldn't he just tell me? I would have respected that. I knew deep down that it was something more, but he should have told me and not let that tramp come at me the way she did. I was very hurt, but I did what Ericka always does and put a smile on my face. You could tell that it wasn't only just effecting me, but me and Tarun's friendship. We didn't talk like we used too, I found myself making all the effort when we did talk, all it was, was pure awkward.

I was so excited about going to Michigan for Thanksgiving, but as the days grew closer I was so afraid. Afraid of the truth, I was afraid to see Kooda face to face, to come so far and go back to fuck up for some bitch all over a nigga. I knew that fighting her wasn't going to solve anything, but hell it was the principle. The fact that she was the one who said she wanted to fight me, when she knew nothing about me. All she knew was what she heard. And if I had a dollar for something that someone had heard, or said about me, hell I coulda paid my way through college.

Jo'Von

What's understood don't need to be explained

If I would have known March 17th 2008 would have been the last time I got to see his face, watch him smile and hear him laugh, I would have had so much more to say to him, I would have made those moments last, I know what Alicia Keys meant when she wrote the song "Like You'll Never See Me Again". I wouldn't have said goodbye because what happens if tomorrow I don't get a chance to say hello again. But what would I say, what would I do? Until the day we meet again all I can do is pray and keep my head up for the both of us, all I can do is hold him down.

I guess you can say with him I do the unthinkable. Most people would call me crazy for having feelings for someone like Jo'Von. But I can't help it and I refuse to let go of what we have because of what people think. People can't make my mind up or change the way I'm feeling. People say that I'm stupid and that I'm a fool for loving a convict, a shooter, a drug dealer and yes maybe I am, but none of those people know what I know about Jo'Von. None of them talk to him like I do, write him and know what's going on in his life like I do. So until they know him like I do they'll never understand.

"Everyday we are faced with difficult situations but have the choice to look at it positively and make the best of it. Nobody knows the future and what tomorrow brings, all we know is how we are left feeling at the end of the day. There are times when I feel like crying but I smile knowing that even though you're not here with me in sight your always with me in everyday I do. You're in my thoughts you're in my prayers you're in my heart and your with me everyday, because I keep your letters in my bag. When I feel down I read those letters because it's you talking to me. I know right now things are bad but babe think of it this way you may be at the bottom but all you can do from here is go up. I know it sounds crazy but it's true because if you never would have gotten locked up I wouldn't have seen you, heard from you, hell we wouldn't have been this close.

I wanna know what are your fears? We all have them but with someone by our side we can overcome them. You wanna know my biggest fear? my fears are that I'm gonna fall even deeper for you than what I already have and won't be able to catch myself, that Imma care for someone who I may never get a chance to see, or to hold you. I'm afraid that I'll never see you and I get hurt.

I love that we are so open and honest with one another. What we have is special and one of a kind. It's indescribable to outsiders but makes perfect sense to us. I've known you a little over a year now but it feels as if it's been longer because we are close. I want you to trust me, to be able to count on me and never doubt me. "All I'm asking you to do is let me hold you down, like a best friend, two homies in the game, when you cry I wanna feel your pain, no secrets no playen. Let me hold you in my arms in my mind all the time I wanna keep you right by my side till I die I'm gonna hold you down and make sure everything is right with you. You can never go wrong if you let me hold you down like a real friends supposed to I'm trying to show you the life of somebody like you should be living oh baby, baby you can never go wrong if you let me hold you down."

Bow   **Wow**

I was glad he was my friend and that deep down I truly cared and had his best interest. Now don't think that that I agree with the choices Jo'Von has made, or the things he has done because I don't he was a sweet kid who got caught up in the wrong mess, the wrong crowd, he got caught up in the world. And now he's paying the price.

Nobody will ever be able to understand what we have, but what's understood don't need to be explained.

Letters from Jo'Von

Bae words can't explain how I feel about you, to me it seems to me that you never kept a secret, always stayed real... Bae I really love you, I enjoy the fact that you care and I feel like you will be my in my future and the love of my life until the end of time. Believe me and take EVERYTHING I say to the heart and understand that I mean every word of it all. I thank you for everything you've done for me.

Everything I do, no matter what it is you're always on my mind. I wonder what you are doing. Are you having fun? Are you being good? And most of all are you safe and outta trouble? Bae "Imma love you when your hair turns grey and I'll still love you if you gain a little weight yea, the way I feel for you will always be the

same just as long as your love don't change. Musiq Soulchild
    I know God don't put too much on us than we can handle. I been in church a lot lately too. I realize the facts of life and I'm making a commitment to myself to change.
    You been there for me since day ONE back in February of 08 and here it is February of 11 Life move like clockwork huh?
    I wanna be with you and only you, you are my backbone you held me down through it all, every smile, every frown, every up and every down through thick and thin, and I thank you for that. For all that you have done for me, I think without you being by my side I don't think I would have made it this far by myself. I love you Ericka LaShawn Newman (Granderson) all them other girls are just jealous girls, the girls that wanna get in my head and screw me over. But I can't take it anymore, my years of being a lady's man is over. It's time to get myself together and focus on getting my diploma
    I feel like you, my grandma and my sister are the closest thing to my heart, and you should feel real special cuz it takes a lot of trust and love for me to open up to anybody and just let them into my heart. I was even thinking about proposing to you, and I'm serious, you asked me what is it I love about you, well I love you! I love your personality, I love the fact you're not afraid to open out to me and that you're by my side holdin me down. I love the visible aspect of you. I love that your open about your feelings and you understand people's ups and downs. That your willing to be there and make sure that everything's taken care of before it even starts, I love that you're willing to support, comfort and make good choices for the both of us.
    I see you stuck on how I was a no show when you asked me to come over on Ribble. Baby I was busy, I had got an invite the same time and funny part about it was I was on Mack St. I never crossed my mind that I was only on the next street over. See back then I was a lil ladies' man and pretty boy but now if you would have asked me to see you I would have stopped everything I was doing and came over.

Imagine.
    Imagine a world where time stands still where nothing you do is at your own free will. Stripped from your freedom and your pride, surrounded by strangers with no place to hide. Imagine a place where you're told what to do, where every choice is made just for you. Surrounded by hate, where all you do is work out and wait. Imagine

a world where u have no voice, a place without reason, a place without choice, a world where you work without much pay and made to feel worthless every day. Image a world where time moves like a snail where all you do is hope for a piece of mail. A world where a meal is eaten just as slow as each day passes. It just makes you sick, imagine a world surrounded by a wire and your freedom is your only desire. If a world like this is hard to conceive then wake up because it's happening to me. I live in this type of world and they won't let me leave. A world where I wish I could turn back the hands of time change my ways and leave this prison life behind wishes are too late when the deed is gone I'm left sitting in prison for what I thought was really fun.

I swear Ericka, you mean everything to me as God as my witness you have no idea how much you mean and what you mean to me. Ericka I don't want nobody but you. I want to be able to be with you and only you, till death do us part. I really want to marry you and I put that on my dead mother. I be telling my man's how he gone be in our wedding and the god father of our three children. I constantly think about you and not a day goes by where I don't bring up your name. I'm willing to do whatever it takes to please you Ericka, I'm serious babe, im not just saying these words because I can, when I said I thought about proposing to you. I want to spend the rest of my life with. No matter what goes on there will be jealous girls throwing dirt on my name, but don't let that change how you feel about me. What is it that made you fall in love with me?

Dear Jo'Von
On April 11th 2011 you wrote me these exact words "Bae I know the feeling when it seems like nobody's there when you're going through all of your problems as if no one cares, well I care. And it took me a while to understand that." Well to be honest I didn't understand what you meant until now. I never really took the time to think about you and what your feeling and what's problems you're facing and have no idea how you are managing to handle it all. And right now you're going through the toughest most difficult time of your life and I been on sum bullshit. Because I promised you I was going to do that. I had been there thru every up down good time and bad and I refuse to start slacking now. But at times it gets hard and

part of me wants to forget but it's like forgetting someone you love is like trying to remember someone you never met. Somedays I tell myself I shoulda tried harder I coulda saved him from all this, but playing the victim isn't going to bring you home and who knows no offense this was the change you needed, you had been saying you wanted to change and get out the streets. In all my letters you told me you felt I was trying to say something and I was but I didn't know the right order to put the words to make you understand or not to hurt you, or not to hurt myself. I been around since February of 08 and look where he at now. I love you, more than words could ever explain, and yea we all get lonely and I tell you everything to how my day was going, to the petty bitches n they drama, to the one night stands because not only are you my best friend but we promised to be real with each other. I'm tired of having boo thangs and late night flights, I want a relationship, a real relationship but I don't know if Im ready to settle down to have to start over to get to know someone all over again, and learn to accept them and trust them, and not have to worry bout them not hurting me. I've been through hell and back and thru all the drama fights bullshit, getting kicked outta school and heartbreak, and shit with my parents, my family, friends and life, I've learned to smile, I look at your pictures and read your letters and I know you're not smiling, I wondering are you praying, and getting closer to God like we should I think about you constantly and though I don't act like it, because I hate getting emotional I hate thinking that there's a possibility that you are not coming home and I'll have to start over, I close my eyes and see your face, and then I'm at peace, because your right where you should be, with me. And those are the days I dreaming is better than reality because the moment I wake up, you'll be gone, you won't be there when I need you, Like I said before I wanna family, three boys and a girl to be exact. I wanna have a successful career and be able to go on trips at least once a year. You told me how you were kinda second guessing getting my name tatted well I'm glad you did, Tatt my name on you so I know it's real, because at first I thought all we had was just prison talk. I'm trying to get back in Wayne

State if not I plan on going to Davenport or Saginaw Valley. I'm getting my life back together; My dad wants me to go back to Jersey but my heart won't let me. I think I'm meant to be in Saginaw and make a difference. This page is going to be the page that's probably going to make you hate me, and upset you and I'm sorry. Remember how you told me not to be out having too much fun while I was in college, Well I behaved myself then, it was once I got to Saginaw in fucked up. I got so caught up in having fun, and going on flights and found out I was 8 weeks pregnant, God didn't feel that it was in his plan for me to have a baby cuz I lost it. I think of it as God telling me I'm meant to be in school making a difference, because you once told me, I'm smart intelligent and capable of great things. Well your capable of great things too, it just took a lot for you to come to that conclusion. All I can say is LET GO and LET GOD. And that means let go of all your worries, problems, emotions, anger, and let God handle it all because like you told me God doesn't take us through more than we can't handle. I love you and though it's hard to smile, you have too, smiling and being at peace gets us through the days when you feel like giving up, and can't take it anymore. Love Always, your go to girl, your rider, your best friend Ericka.

Bryson

Bryson Tiller said "Girl he only fucked you over cuz you let him" and honestly that's exactly what happened. Someone fucked me over because I allowed him too. So does that make me an idiot, I ask myself was it really his fault? He only did what I allowed him to do to me, so anything that happened am I to blame? Do I accept full responsibility? I put the blame on Bryson for years because it was easier to blame him for the things that went wrong. Nobody ever really wants to admit their own guilt. He was a much easier pill to swallow that he was an asshole, and that it was his fault. But in all actuality once I got older and started evaluating my life and everything that happened I can only blame myself. Because once again people only do what you allow them too. And i allowed myself to settle, settling being the side bitch, settling to come second, i allowed myself to be used, to be a lustful encounter whenever and wherever he wanted. I allowed myself to be available for him, any day, anywhere, any time.

I always questioned and wondered how could this happen? how could this go on for so long? Because I allowed it, that's why. Never once did I say I didn't want to play these games anymore, never once did i speak up and say what I was willing and not willing to accept. My heart caught feelings that my mind told me I should have. I felt like I knew exactly what R.Kelly meant when he said "My minds telling me no but my body, my body's telling me yes!" I let my hormones control every sense of my mind and body. And all i could think about was how amazing I heard he was in bed. Getting a piece of that chocolate. that late night snack you crave, that you know you shouldn't have but you get it anyway.

But answer me this! How would you handle and deal with when you initially were just lustful of one another and it turns into actually getting to know one another? How many of ya'll ever had that one person that you vibe with hard as fuck can talk to him about whatever but everything is based off sex? I could sit and talk to him for hours, laugh joke and just be myself. But at the end of the day I knew the deal. His girl was his Monday thru Friday, I just kept him satisfied thru the weekend. sometimes I would dip and dive on a Tuesday or Thursday, fuck around and call him on Monday or late Wednesday. But I knew what he wanted, I knew what he came for. And i knew he stayed around for years because I knew what he wanted and how he wanted it. I knew what he liked, what turned him on. sometimes I even would tell myself he stayed around cuz deep down he might have liked me too, that he actually might have cared, and after all the shit i put him thru he had to have gave somewhat of a fuck cuz he shoulda just been left me alone. But i fucked all that up cuz back then I didn't know how to shut the fuck up keep a good thing going, and just kept my mouth shut.

You ever had that feeling of wanting to share your good news? Ever just had tea you had to spill? Have you ever had that moment of pettiness to let the next bitch know like NANANA BOO BOO bitch, his bitch tried to play me like I was just an average basic ass bitch. That I was the type of bitch her nigga would never dare in a million years fuck, or I was just and only that a fuck that happened once or twice when they was on bad terms. Well ya'll must have been on bad terms forever cuz lil baby like me was always in the picture. Tried to play it like her nigga wouldn't even look in my direction, but yet I'm knocking his socks off. Legs wrapped around his neck and shoulders, scratching his back throwing it back on the same dude you swore wouldn't even give me the time a day? HMM how sway sis, tell me how that work?? I wanted her to feel salty as fuck.

I was young and dumb back then, i was proud to be the side bitch. I was proud to say even tho he ain't mines is he really yours? Kash Doll said "He ain't gone ever love a square bitch, baby girl you gone have to share him." But he had the type of bitch that if you talking that shit you better be ready to fight. She'd pull up on you ANYWHERE! "You talking that shit but bae must i remind you I am that bitch I will pull up and find you" was the kinda bitch he had. She was all about her nigga, "he might be for everybody but she was who that motherfucker belonged too" and he wasn't going nowhere. And a while back I saw someone post "IF YOU KEEP HAVING TO CONFONT YOUR DUDE ABOUT THE SAME CHICK THEN ITS MORE TO IT THEN JUST A ONE NIGHT STAND. HE HAS SOME SORT OF INVESTMENT WITH HER SOME SORT OF FEELINGS FOR HER.

And in the back of my mind that was exactly how I felt. We had good chemistry, got along great and the sex was fan fucking tastic. He was east to talk to and I was easy to listen and understand. And whenever he had a long stressful day I seemed to help take all that away I helped make him forget about the shitty day he had. Any frustrations or anger he had he took it out on me and not in a bad way if you catch my drift. We were always so honest with one another, he was with his main bitch and I was with a nigga. Like "Aye now's not a good time I'll hit you up later type shit." and I respected it because he coulda flat out lied or been sneaking and geekin actin weird and shit.

So why the nigga who always kept it so honest start fucking lying out the blue?? You talk about a confused bitch that shit set me back. Went from yea i know everything there is to know about that nigga to hell I swear he switched up cuz ion know this motherfucker before me. Went from I know the nigga, to I don't know why I even fuck with the nigga. He started to do little dumb shit, but the thing that took the cake was when he started fucking my friends and lying about it. You ain't never lied to me about nothing you did or do so why start now. My vision of you was once so clear was now cloudy and doubtful. I think that bastard fucked about a good three or four of my homegirls, and the only reason why i was mad was when confronted him(confronting him like he was my nigga tho) he straight up lied to my face. And the one thing i hate more than anything is to be lied too cuz I feel like I'm not worth the truth. Oh well, if the truth is gonna hurt but I rather know deal with it and move on. He told me altho I wanted the truth I couldn't handle it. Well apparently I could handle the lies either, cuz that's when I started getting outta pocket. That's when I stopped giving a fuck and got ignorant. All that keep what we doing on the hush, nope imma shout it off the roof top tell anyone about you who's willing to listen, cuz the worse thing that's gone happen is you gone cuss me out and leave me alone, but I bet you know don't fucking play with me.

My point on it is this. I don't want to knowingly fuck behind anyone. Especially not none of my damn friends. Hell only way I'll willingly share him is if I'm having a threesome and I'm too selfish for that kind of hoohahh. Everybody keeps saying how small Saginaw is you bound to fuck with somebody that somebody you know used to fuck with. And be that as it may, if we still fucking and you tell me this my dick, that my pussy yours and I can't fuck no other dude. Why you get to be like public transportation giving everyone a free ride? It don't work like that. I will politely let the bitch you wanna fuck gone head and have you.

It's a level of respect, but is that my karma for not respecting what he had going on? But damn my friends tho, fuck a bitch that don't got no connection or ties to me cuz imma feel like you met them thru me and when we was sneaking n geeking you had ya eyes on something else. But foolish young dumb me, I couldn't leave that boy alone. I couldn't shake em even if you paid me too, or tried to beat my ass, run me over and kill me. Couldn't stop fucking with him even if my relationship was on the line. And today I ask myself after all you been thru, after all you've seen and done. After all the hurt, pain, and tears why the fuck didn't you cut all ties?

To be honest, I just wasn't ready. I could change my number a numerous of times and he'd still get it. I could say I was done and wanted him to get his act together or I could cut him off for a while. But always found his way back to my side door. Found his way back in my texts and call logs at any given time of night. I guess I tried to just stay down for him. I was around when everybody else had come and gone. I had prayed for the little bastard more than I did myself. Prayed that he would one day see how I had his back even if he didn't have mine. I would pray that he had a good day and if he had a bad one the angels would watch over him, I prayed that everytime he was out in the streets he would make it home safely.

Everything is all fun and games until you get pregnant! And especially when it's a baby that he doesn't want. You may think you know how a man feels about you, but you never truly know until you could potentially be the mother of their child. You could have all the history, chemistry and good vibes in the world. But all that history and connection you thought you had, chemistry and good vibes were just fun and good time.

Now one time I can maybe somewhat agree with, cuz sometimes you not ready and you fuck up kids just ain't in the cards for ya'll. But when you dodge a bullet like that, be grateful and move the fuck on with your life. Don't keep back tracking reminiscing on all the old times and let him find his way to your bed again Cuz I put money on it you'll get pregnant again. Don't be stupid, don't be foolish and be like Ericka and get pregnant again. Cuz that's when the I'm not ready for another baby speech. I'm just now getting it together with the one I got. Part of you wants to respect the fact that he's honest but then again I was insulted. This was the way I looked at it "I'm good enough to fuck unprotected when you and I both know the consequences. I'm good enough to get the you wanna have my baby during sex talk but when I say yea and end up pregnant It's like OMG the fucking world is about to end type shit. I can't wrap my head around the shit. but it was like his word was law and what he said goes. And while I sat in the parking lot and those protesters banged on my car and got my second guessing what I was about to do. Hearing them yell I was going to burn in hell I was afraid. But I already had a baby that wasn't even a year old yet, and I can't handle another one. As bad i as mentally tried to tell myself that i wanted this baby so bad. I wanted that baby with everything in me because that baby was a part of him.

I kept playing in my head that he said he wasn't ready for more kids and that little dirty dick bastard had three more so what was the big deal with me? What did they have that I didn't? The power to say they was keeping they kid? Did he love them? And it hurt even worse to see those kids every day. Or at an event, at the park. Being reminded that these were the kids that he wanted. I broke down and felt sorry for myself for so long. Somedays it still hurts like it happened yesterday. and when I see him and he tells me how much he loves them and his kids are his world and he's so glad he's their dad I be wanting to tell him to shut the fuck up and how dare you. Did you forget or not realize who you are having this conversation with? I had to let that hurt go! Had to let all that pain and anger go. Kind of hard to feel some type of way and have animosity towards the mad you hit from time to time. But remember people only do what you allow them too.

Courtney

So, I've always been told "people make time for who and what they want to make time for" Do you believe that? Me personally, I most definitely agree one thousand percent. There's no if ands or butts about it. There's not one person extremely that busy to where they can't make a 20 second phone call or send a quick text. Now I understand not being able to just sit on the phone and chit chat, cuz that's a broke man's hustle but with that same phone you're going live with, posting statuses, tweeting, posting pics for IG and Sap Chat you can go to your messages and just say hey, don't gotta be nothing to major. Nor do every time we talk, we have to talk about going somewhere or doing something.

No man is busy, every second, of every minute of every hour of the day. Hell I got a life, I'm a mom of a 5-year-old and an infant, work a steady 9-5, and have to find the time to do mommy and daughter things, be a good girlfriend to a boyfriend if I had one. Still be a good sister, daughter and friend and find the time for a social life. Got back in school, take care of home, cooking cleaning, paying bills (now mind you thee are responsibilities I took on when I became a mother and adult and they are things as a woman I am supposed to do so I don't complain) and yet I still made the time to first come up with these thoughts turn them into words on paper to my laptop to write this book, now that that's time!

If I like you, I'm gonna try my best to fit you into wherever I got going on. Imma make sure to include you and if I'm invested I you put forth that effort, that time and investment. That's why I be so pissed when these lil fuckboys waste my time and they wonder why I be out here being a savage and shit. I'm the type of girl, I love affection and attention (now don't confuse it with that clingy being all extra with the PDA) and I know we all got lives so we don't have to be together 24/7 just laid up like we aint got shit to do. But I like my dude to be like GM Babe, occasionally let me sleep in and cook me breakfast type shit. Or notice like you got on my favorite perfume or even I like what you did to your hair. To notice the little ass shit! Nothing to major. I love the thought of knowing I'm yours, your mine! I rather spend time than money. Hell we can pull up to Wendy's and get a four for four pull up to the park with a blanket and some music take the kids and turn it into a family fun day and I'd be happy.

My Facebook friend Corey asked "Would you rather have a nigga spend time and not really have no money? Or have money and spend no time? I gave ya'll my take on it already, but I saw so many ladies responding that they rather have a dude with money. And I wanted to say how shallow, childish, ignorant and scandalous can you be? Is what a man got and can give you more important than spending time? I mean don't get it twisted having a man who is financially stable and has the funds to do whatever whenever and when you're in a bind to have a "Nate" around. And I hope it doesn't come across hoesish and hypercritical when I say I shouldn't be fucking no nigga that I can't call in case of an emergency anyways!

Now let's be clear. I make and have my own and emphasis on own money and rely on myself, but there are times when we all myself included fall short. And if I'm at work and forgot to bring lunch or call and ask you for 20$ or I need a jump or a ride or anything what am I fucking you for? You little dirty dick bastards don't be afraid to ask me for m no money or no ride, a place to sleep house and store ya shit and most defiantly don't be afraid to ask for no pussy. So why should I be afraid to ask for anything? Females be so afraid to ask a dude for something cuz they think they gone say no or look at them like they need them, but fail to realize now a days dudes will sell you a dream and rob you blind fuck you and sometimes the dick ain't even worth a quarter dry text you and leave you.

Any who I've gotten a little of topic and away from my point, I can't stress the importance enough of the fact that any dude can give you penis, but can he give you his time? I don't want someone slanging dick like community property and public restrooms. I want someone who's devoted and into me. I mean fellas how hard is it to be honest? Tell me what I need to know and not what you want me to think or wanna hear! Don't do boyfriend shit, if you're not boyfriend material. Ya'll be wanting a girl who cooks cleans washes ya clothes supports ya dreams, goes to school and work, is a great mom have no niggas, be in shape, be a freak, answer whenever you can and reply quickly to texts, help you secure the bag, put her dreams on hold to help support you. Be fashionable, and always on fleek. But what do you have to offer? Beside McDonalds 2 for 2 money some musty dick, the same jogging suit you had on for about 4 days and prolly didn't wash your ass don't know how to cook, and didn't finish school. You mother fuckers sicken me!

Sorry, thinking too much off emotions right now!

Me personally I've had more fun with dudes who really ain't have much, those were some of the guys I've had the most enjoyable time with. They were humble. (At least most of them) They remembered the struggle, what it was like to want and dream and made sure that every day they made it count. You got some of these "yeah I got it niggas, be flashy for IG, Snap, and Facebook but in real life, couldn't even buy you a double cheeseburger meal, can't support your habits let alone they own.

I've come across some who should never have any money cuz they don't fucking know what to do with it. Spend it on these bitches, ball on these niggas but can't break bread with they BM. Don't support they children, but got all the latest and greatest, Jordan's, I-phones but still living in they mama basement ass niggas.

I've been telling myself I wanted a guy off into the church, for a long while now, and although I was bullshitting around but seriously I think that I'm going to have to give it a try. Not saying that I need me a man, so I can change and improve my life, but it helps get you motivated and every now and again we all need a little tug, and push. I'm ready to take that leap of faith head first in a direction I've never walked before. Trying the whole walk by faith and not by sight type of thing.

I'm learning that everything that glitters ain't gold and everything I want I don't need. I'm learning to humble myself and just be grateful for what I have cuz some people might not think of it as much and it might mean so much to someone else. So you never know if someone's looking at your life half empty.

Have you ever had someone in your life make you become a better you? Make you want to do a whole 360 on your life? If you want something bad enough your gonna go get it! And I'm not trying to hear the by any and all means shit. You ain't gotta rob, cheat and steal. You don't have to step on toes and do people dirty.

Courtney was that friend that I always wanted to make sure he saw me at my best, but I guess he couldn't see in me what I wanted him too, and like I said the older I've gotten, I'm not gone beat a dead horse or keep giving cpr to dead situations.

Virginity

Virginity can be lost by a thought

Time to back track for a minute and go back to the very beginning, some of you are probably wondering why I didn't start off with this. Well not all stories are meant to be in order, sometimes in order to see where someone is going you have to see where they've been. I was trying to figure out myself how did I get to this point. I believe you learn and get a better understanding of someone when you know what they have been through. People act according to the things they've been through, overcome, and haven't yet conquered yet. Packing up and moving on is easy, it's the unpacking and getting your life back on track that's the hard part. Its like I have all my bags and am ready to unpack them and get on with my life, but each piece of luggage holds a painful memory and as much as I want to forget about it all, it's made me who I am today, and I'm scared that all those memories good or bad, will come back, and I'll be in the very same place, that I just left from.

I never much really talked about the day I lost my virginity, never told a soul really, it was like I blocked it out of my memory, or it just never happened. But even when you try to forget, it's still there, it's there when you wake up, when you go to sleep. You're reminded when you get into a new relationship, in your thoughts is this guy like that guy that was just like the first guy. Am I going to care for him and he gone not just screw me physically but mentally, and emotionally? You have this wall and your scared that once someone gets to close that all that building is going to go to waste and all those years you spent preparing yourself was plain dumb.

A moment in time that's supposed to be just a meaningful as the day you turn 16, 18, 21 or your wedding day. A moment that was ruined, and was only your fault, because you let it get to this point of no turning back, and you can't face it, you look in the mirror and sometimes you hold back the tears and other days you don't care who you let see the tears fall.

I walked passed him hoping and praying he knew who I was. I knew exactly who he was. I spotted him out a mile away, To this day, I still remember the way he smells, the roughness and manliness of the touch of his hands. The moment I heard his voice I could never forget the face of the boy I lost my virginity too. In a way it's a shame that some people can have sex with someone and months later, hell even years can pass and they look at you like you're a total stranger.

Was I a stranger? Was it that he forgot about me, or he just didn't care to remember?

I wanted to speak to him but what was I too say? When I passed him by did he glance and in the back of his mind did he think that girl looks familiar, is that such and such? I wanted to speak to him but what was I too say? Oh hey, know you probably don't remember me but you took my virginity a couple years back, I wanted you too know that I think you're a fucken jerk, you ruined my life and I hate your freaking guts, well that's all I wanted it was so nice seeing you again?

Sitting across the room, I could hear their whispers about the new girl. I even heard one tell another boy about the things he wanted to do to me if he ever had the chance, fucken pervert. I saw the girls look at me with such hatred, such envy, because I was stealing the attention that they wanted. I couldn't help but laugh because it was clear as day they were jealous and jealousy's the ugliest trait. Sitting across the room, by myself I could hear people trying to be friendly, but they just wanted to be noisy.

I could see him, watching, how gently I crossed my legs, how smoothly I licked my lips, and most of all how innocently I smiled. I knew as he stared he couldn't help but wonder if I was a virgin or not. I left it up to his imagination, to have him walk past me, too look and smile too know that I was a fish he couldn't catch. I left him to fantasize to have his moment because in his mind he could do whatever, but in reality all he could do was look.

I heard someone tell me to come here, I turned around and it was Jay. He said his homeboy Louie wanted to talk too me. I smiled and said if he wants too talk to me tell him to come over here and talk to me. I didn't need someone being a messenger, don't have someone else come do your dirty work for you, do it yourself.

Louie, the first boy I met at Ruben Daniels. Louie a real cute Hispanic brotha, with a couple of tattoos, a little mustache, beard, and a mole on his face. He was 16 years old still in the 8th grade, I thought I was funny that I was 12 and in the 7th grade and at the rate Louie was going he would be in the 8th grade again next year. He told me that I had a baby face, looked way younger than 12, looked so innocent. I remembered he told he how I wasn't like those other girls, how I didn't let these boys get to me. That I wasn't too grown for my age, that there was something about my smile that made me special that made me stand out.

Louie told me he wanted to make me scream, make me moan and feel like I never felt before, I got all warm inside at the thought. He pulled me closer to him as he rubbed my shoulders. He pulled me to him, kissed me and I pushed away. I gripped his face closer towards mine, could feel him breathing out the air I was breathing in, my heart trembled and my lips quivered, I was shacking, I couldn't help but feel as if what I was doing was wrong but inside it couldn't help but feel right. He kissed my forehead, my neck then my collarbone, sucked on my nipples until they were rock hard. He kissed my stomach and stopped at my belly button

Louie: *"We cant fight what the body desires. You can try and fight the temptation but it only makes you want it more."*

As he pulled me closer I could tell he was ready but me not so much but I didn't want too seem like a punk. I started something that deep down I knew I wasn't ready to finish, but I couldn't stop here. I wouldn't have just been teasing him but I'd be teasing myself. I wanted him to stop, but in the same breath I wanted him to keep going. He told me times like this stop meant go and no meant yes. I didn't know what anything meant at that point so I just laid there helpless, out of mind out of body praying it would be over soon.

Two bodies clenched together, bonded by sweat and temptation. He said he knew it was right, the moment he saw the tears trickling down my face. He could see the pain in my eyes and not an ounce of compassion. Looking up at him, I wandered did he want me? Want me the same way I wanted him as more than just someone to fuck? I liked him but I knew I liked him for the wrong reasons, I liked his swag, I loved that beautiful Mexican skin, the mole on his face, the accent in his voice, and the fact that someone actually gave me the time of day. The way I felt at that very moment I was willing, willing to do whatever I could to make, him happy, to make him stay, to make this feeling last, because I never felt a feeling like this.

I wonder what would have happened if I would have ever had the "sex talk" with my parents. It would have been so awkward, but in the end greatly appreciated. I learned the hard way that boys will say whatever they have too, to get what they want. They'll tell you how pretty you are even when you look the worse, they'll say they love you when the could really careless, will call you everyday and once they get some ass their gone with the wind, and you feel like you have to search high and low and damn near stalk them just to say hello. Had my mind so far gone, I couldn't find it even if it was standing right in front of my face. I actually believed that there was something when there was absolutely nothing.

We hadn't known one another that long, only a couple of weeks and in my mind I felt foolish I felt stupid but Louie told me nothing was wrong with what we were doing as long as I liked him and wanted him the same way he liked and wanted me.

Fifty-seven minutes later, my innocence was gone.

I remember lying there confused because I was told you have sex with the person you loved, and I didn't love Louie. Hell I hardly even knew him. He did love me, he lusted for me. My virginity taken by a boy I barley knew anything about, by a boy who the kids in my class told me was no good. Taken by a boy who only wanted to bust a nut. No longer did I feel clean I felt dirty, and no matter how long I scrubbed I couldn't wash it off. I couldn't get rid of his smell his touch, his voice was stuck inside my head.

After that night, I saw Louie everyday in school but we never spoke, never even look at one another. But I felt as if everybody was looking at me, everybody knew that I had sex with Louie and deep down they were laughing at me, silent laughter never sounded so loud. I could hear them whisper and I wanted to tell them all to just shut the fuck up and mind their business. Ruben Daniels had no secrets, everybody knew everything about everyone who entered those doors. I felt so embarrassed because my private life had never been so open.

I was so happy when I left Ruben Daniels, I ran away and never went back. Too many people, too many rumors, that I couldn't handle or control Too many painful memories, the place where I lost my virginity, my sanity and my innocence.

I still cant believe that he couldn't recall my face, I was face to face with a total stranger. As I walked past him he smiled and waved trying to get my attention but there was nothing I had too say too him. He didn't even know me and that was worst than fifty slaps in the face.

Louie: *Don't I know you from somewhere? I mean you look so familiar but I cant recall where I know you from for the life of me.*

Ericka: *No I don't believe so.*

It wasn't that much I remembered about Louie or Ruben Daniels, the only thing that comes to my mind when you bring up either one was that was a time in my life that happened a long time ago. I was young and I'm older now, mistakes happen but it's those very mistakes that mold you, that can either make you or break you.

I was absolutely right when I said Louie never knew me, because he didn't. He knew nothing about me as I knew nothing about him. It wasn't that much I remembered about Louie or Ruben Daniels, the only thing that comes to my mind when you bring up either one was that was a time in my life that happened a long time ago. I was young and I'm older now, mistakes happen but it's those very mistakes that mold you, that can either make you or break you.

I hear stories about girls who are still til this day in love with the boy the lost their virginity too, then I hear stories from girls like me. Girls who's first was just a one night stand, they don't speak and when they do see one another they act as if the others invisible. They have so many hateful feelings towards that person. Why couldn't me and Louie be friends? Why did it have to turn out the way it did?

If I could go back in time I'd of never had sex with Louie. We were complete strangers. There was a big ass age difference between the two of us and I would have made my first time special. The hardest thing to swallow is once it got out it spread like wild fire. Louie was around the same age as my uncle, they hung around the same crowd and one day he confronted me on it. I was in total shock I didn't want to tell my uncle that I was having sex. My uncles crazy, just like my momma and I wasn't trying to get my ass beat I'm too smart for that. So with a very simple no I walked away and told him too never bring it up again. I told him that boys lie and you shouldn't believe everything you hear. But the only person lying was me, and I was only lying to myself.

For the longest time I think I believed that nothing had ever happened between Louie and I.

Getting dumped and Getting over it

If someone you love hurts you cry a river, build a bridge, and get over it.

I've never been able to handle getting dumped. I'm the kinda girl if I'm annoyed or mad everyone else has to be too. I'll blow a nigga phone up, I'll call private and leave nasty yet funny little messages. I don't give a flying fuck or a rat's ass, I advise you not to leave nothing at my crib. Not a tooth brush, not a comb, no deodorant, no shoes, not a got damn thing, because if you piss me off I'm going to do bad things to your shit. Yes, it's petty and childish but I'm just being honest.

Getting dumped is one tough pill to swallow but it happens to everyone. Even to the people who think they are incapable of it ever happening to them. It happens to those people who think that they are in love. It happens to the best of us so put on your big girl panties and prepare yourself for it. It happens over thirty second phone calls, emails, texts, and voicemail and now Facebook. Sadly now days it never happens face to face. Getting over an ex is hard but you need to realize that it's over and you need to stop living in the past. It's okay to cry but not to feel sorry for yourself, because that's not going to get him back. Throw away all the letters and pictures because holding on to old memories bring back a lot of pain. Let it go because time heals all wounds, the pain and hurt won't last forever.

Why? Who knows why and why it happened doesn't matter. All that matters is the one you once called your boyfriend has left you for someone else and there's nothing you can do about it. We get so caught up and tend to blame ourselves on why it happened. Was I not doing what he wanted, did he want more or less? Did I come off to strong or not strong enough? Was I clingy or too distant? They say what one wont do, another one will..

It's hard seeing your ex with someone new. A lot of the time it's just in a girls nature to have hatred towards the new girlfriend. But I personally don't understand why. I look at it this way maybe the best thing you did was let him go. If you couldn't make him happy let him be with someone who can. There's no point in holding a grudge towards her because she didn't do anything wrong, unless she was ya best friend and if she was they say don't bring ya man around ya girls cuz females will do you dirty in a heartbeat just because they don't want to see you happy. Even if your man left you for your ex best friend that's spilled milk and there's no point in crying over spilled milk.

You don't have to remain friends but don't let bad blood take control over your life because they only person you're really hurting is yourself.

I ask people why is it that men cheat? Most would say because men are low down dirty bustards with no compassion toward our feelings. And be that as it may that it may have some truth to it but truth be told it's the very same reason why women cheat. Because they can, and because they can they want too and there is always someone willing to cheat with them. No ones ever sorry for cheating if they were they wouldn't be cheating in the first place. No one's ever sorry for what they do while they're doing it. They only become remorseful once they get caught. And the only reason is not that they cheated but they got caught, that they were slick enough to get away with it. Because I know if I could get away with it I wouldn't be sorry.

The one thing I hate more than anything, is when someone tells me that I deserve better. If that's the case, you knew you had no good intentions so why even bother in the first damn place? The worst thing you can tell me right now is that I can find someone better, when I thought I had already found the best. To tell me to forget you, it's impossible, like trying to remember someone I've never met. To have someone say that what we had was special, if it was so special why the fuck are you ending it? To watch someone pretend as if I don't even exist. I cant pretend to be happy, I can fake a smile, and pretend I'm fine but the one thing I can't fake, pretend or hide was that I cared for you.

The hardest part of dreaming about someone you love is having to wake up. The worst way to love someone is to sit next to them, knowing they don't love you back. You don't realize how much you care about someone until they don't care about you. The hardest thing you'll ever watch is watching the one you love, love someone else. All of these things can be overcome the moment you stop crying over the past, and when you stop beating yourself up and putting all the blame on you.

To All The Boys That Lost Me

It's like you have no clue how many nights or how long I've sat there, crying myself to sleep, or how many nights I've sat there and thought about you wondering what are you doing? Are you thinking of me? Have you just moved on? Is this really it? Because when a heart break no it don't break even. You don't quite understand how many times I've put you in my prayers, I pray for you more than anyone else, that one day you get it. I pray that the feelings I felt I will go away, that they'll never come back and I'll get over you.

You don't even care about the damaged you've caused and that broken hearts don't heal that easily. It's like your not even sorry for screwing with my head, my emotions or my heart. For coming and going whenever you please. Leaving me to wait for when you returned. For you times going by but for me it's standing still. Because when a heart break no it don't break even. You don't even care about the promises you made, let alone about the promises you've broken. Or the fact that I haven't broken any of mine, because I don't say things I don't mean

It's like you shut the door in my face, yet for you my door is always open. When you need me I'll cross the ocean to get too you and when I need you, you leave me waiting like a lil kid in the rain who just missed the bus. You left me in the rain, cold and alone with no where to go. Why is it im the one left with all the tears? why is it me who still cares? why can't I get over you because it's clear your over me? Because when a heart break no it don't break even.

I thank you, yes I thank you, I wanna thank you, for making me a woman –Estelle You all have all molding me into the woman I am today. I took all of these unfortunate encounters as life lessons. Lessons I will take with me the rest of my life. No need to cry no need to feel down and unworthy, because I now know my worth. You all have given me what I was unable to give myself all these years. I found a sense of self! I wasn't aware of what I was willing to put up and deal with until I got myself into. I am the woman I am today because of you, all of you, and isn't it ironic how things work. The same female that you played and fucked over is the same girl you acting like Biggie begging for one more chance. Ya'll see the glow up, you see in me in a spot that not even I thought possible. All my life I had to fight like Sophia from the color purple, but I have no more fight left in me.

Now one thing I can say, in all yall defense that we were young and didnt have the knowledge and experience we have now about relationships, but young or not, you don't do someone the way you did me, that's just wrong. You wouldn't want anyone to do your mother, sister or daughter that way. Well look at it like this, im someones mother, daughter and sister. Did I deserve that? Lets face it, you only did what I allowed you to, I gave you that power, but I wont allow it anymore.

There were days, I prayed for you, more than I prayed for myself. Prayed that God would protect you, watch over you and would guide your heart and change your ways. Guess I was praying for the wrong things. Because I asked God to watch over me, to heal my heart, repair my mind body and soul, to remove negativity from my life. When he saw that I was ready to focus on me. He removed all of you sons of bitches from my life, some ended badly, and some not so much, but the fact of the matter is that when you are ready to accept what God his telling you. Stop following your own path and trust in the Lord with all thy heart and lean not of your own understanding. Commit your way to the Lord, trust in him, he will do it, won't he do it!!

Somebody's gonna love me one day, love the shit outta me, love every flaw, every attitude every little thing about me. Their gonna love the spirit and energy, I have. Their gonna love, what I can do and what I can bring to the table. I'm gonna get me someone who loves the woman I am, accept the woman I was and help mold me into the woman I want to become. Not being funny, I hope you all get what you deserve, whatever that may be. You go searching for a woman you want to change control or use and you're gonna get exactly what you ask for, and your gonna hate it. Your gonna get you a woman who aint shit, aint bout shit, aint gone never be shit or amount to shit, because she's cool with whee she's at in life. I hope you fall in love with a bitch who plays the fuck outta you. I hope you expreince the worst heartbreak that your heart cant handle.

Yeah, it might be petty, it might be childish, and I should do the righteous thing, and wish you well, and the best of luck and all the happiness in the world because wishing you anything other than that makes me sound mad, bitter and jealous. No not really, that's just me giving you real and raw unedited feedback and emotions. That be the problem with so many of us now a days we say things we don't mean, ty to be polite fuck all that, im over the nice phase, yes I've moved on, yes im content happy all that but do you know how long it took me to get this way.. So let me feel the way that I feel.

I cant pretend that everything's okay, I cant bite my tongue

117

and walk away, I cant pretend that I'm not hurt, I cant forget that you lied, I cant forget all those nights I held my pillow and cried....I used to think that I needed you but really I need myself. For all of you who lost me, I know you're glad in some way that you met me and won't ever forget me and some will be calling me very soon. I'm going to tell you something I never thought I'd be able to say, I forgive you. Even though you hurt me, it's okay. I see how you all are living your lives and its time I live mine. I pray for you and still do till this day that God will forever bless you and watch over you, the way he has done for me.

Please don't lie, please don't cheat, please be gentle and please be sweet. Please don't break my heart, please don't take me for a fool, please don't diss me thinking it's cool. Please love me and don't think of me as something to do, please don't hurt me cuz I won't hurt you. Please be mindful that I have feelings please don't use me as no rebound cuz in the name of Karma what goes around comes around.

I was looking for LOVE in all the wrong places. I searched high and low settled for relationships that were no good because I didn't want to be lonely. Then one day I stopped searching and love found me. It's amazing we are completely oblivious to what's standing there right in front of our faces waiting for us all this time.

"Life isn't measured by the number of breaths we take, but by the moments that take our breath away"

Where Are They Now??

I and my mom are trying to restart our new mother and daughter relationship but things like that don't happen overnight. Sometimes it takes years to accomplish but we go one step at a time each and everyday. We had to just start over because there was no fixing, restoring, repairing, or mending what we had. What was it I wanted from my mother? Was it that I wanted her to say "look I messed up and I'm sorry?" I wanted her to feel my pain my hurt, anger and confusion. Or was it that I simply wanted her to hug me. But you know what she did say to me. That she was proud of me that she was seeing a change in me and most of all that she loved me and right then I broke. Because that's all I ever wanted. I never meant to have a unstable and unhealthy relationship with the woman who gave birth and raised me. I wanted to be the daughter she raised the daughter she expected me to be.

"Mommy I am so sorry that it had to get to this point, to have you disappointed because I never meant to hurt you, I guess no one ever really means to hurt anyone but I let my selfish ways get in the way and I hope you forgive me. I know we'll never be the same we'll be better, we'll be able to sit in the same room, be able to talk and laugh, to agree and most importantly I'll be able to appreciate you and give you the love and respect you deserve."

Last I heard about Edrick was that was living in Midland playing step daddy with some 30 something year old lady and her four or five kids. I haven't talked to him in months and you know what it doesn't bother me {but it does just a little because if I didn't I wouldn't have brought it up} We are both living our lives now, and we don't dwell in the past. I don't concern myself thinking could we have made it. It's the past and I'm finally putting it behind me. I sit and smile at what we had because at least we got to share it, we can never get it back, replace it or to and fix it. I still had the old photos but they didn't make me cry like before. He's always in my prayers that he's safe and happy. I finally gave up and it wasn't because I was weak it was because I was finally strong enough to let go.

I think I held on for as long as I possibly could, the thing about it was that though he was older than me we both were young, and yes we claim we wanted something more, but we were way in over our heads, Yes I love Edrick we shared three years together. Yes they were rough and complicated years but hey, we all grow, some of us grow up and some of us grow apart. Deep down I really believed that there was hope for us, but I know a long time ago that it was over, I just didn't want to believe it or speak it because you have what you say.

Something's fall out of order so other things can fall into place I guess.

His girlfriend is so childish, you'd think she's younger than me. She called me at 2;59 in the morning playing on my phone. Telling me how happy Edrick and she were and that I need to leave him alone. She said I was crazy and obsessed. Obsessed, not at all, but in love I was and you can't turn your feelings on and off. But he called me not too long ago and I didn't know how to feel about it. I was happy to hear from him but then again it was probably better off that I hadn't. So I finally threw those old photos away because the held no purpose, only pain.

No Privacy

Scooter's still the same old bastard he was when I first met him and now I think I hate him more. He doesn't respect me and now he never will. Deep down I still miss him just a little because it was just so fun but the fun must end somewhere. He got a girl named Vanessa and she got him tatted. I wish them the best of luck, but I wonder how long it will last cuz Scooter can't be faithful, probably wouldn't know faithful if it sucked his dick and treated him like a king. One thing I liked about her that I couldn't deny, she did have a lil feistiness in her, I'll give it to Scooter sure knew how to pick em. I heard through very reliable sources that she didn't like me and wanted to fight me, but that shit aint faze me. She's a lil ass girl in that young love stage and she gone fight for what's hers. But I feel like this if you knew ya part you wouldn't be worrying about an old bitch.

We actually got kind of cool, she's not that bad, she's crazy as hell but aren't we all in our own little way? She's bout to have his baby, and part of me is happy, part of me wishes her the best, and majority of me prays for her because that shit aint gone be easy. And I hate to admit it that part of me is and was jealous.

Dale is probably still with Passion hell if I know, He was my dirty little secret but I finally did my laundry. He was the drug I was addicted to so I checked myself into rehab. I still get tingles whenever I see him and I tend to flashback to the good old days. As for Zoe he's gone with the wind has been for sometime now. And just when you think you have finally let it go, there it is standing right back in your face, when you least expect it, and have to control your feelings because your in public. I ran into Zoe three days before Christmas at the Celebration Hall, and all I could think was DAMN!!!! He looks even better than I last remembered. We hung out one day and everything was all good. Told me that he missed me and how his mama asked about me, and we talked about the good ol days, and for a moment, I got caught slippin, I honestly thought, we had a good thing going, but somethings are just too good to be true. Zoe had a girlfriend, and once again I was left feeling dumb.

Quason's still my unsolved puzzle and I think its best if I never solve it. I love his little sister to death, and even if there's no more Quason and I she will still be my little sister. I couldn't buy my way to his heart because all it did was make me bitter and broke. I tried and tried but then you get to a point to where you get tired of trying when you keep getting the same results at the end of the day.

July 20, 2010, he asked me what was it I wanted to do and until he asked me I always thought I knew, but now I don't. I know what I want to do but I'm afraid of the outcome. It's like I don't really wanna go, but he don't really wanna stay, we need to just make up our minds and get it together. Deep down yes I care for him but the question is does he care for me?

Now I'm at a point to where I don't know what to do anymore. I still want us too be friends and be able to call one another jus to say hi and see how the others been but I doubt it. One day he called me and it was the most awkward conversation ever, we sat there just breathing, and like usual I had to start the conversation. He went on to say he didn't believe me nor did he trust me, when just a couple of weeks ago it was something totally different. It made me sad but then again why even call or try and fake it anymore. That hurt me more than anything because there's an us in trust and without trust there is no us. I tried my hardest to always keep it real with Quason but there came a point when I had to start not only thinking of him but myself.

I know the reason he didn't trust me had everything to do with me and Tarun? It's so hard to get to tomorrow when yesterday keeps pulling me back. When I sit and think about today there's something in the back of my mind that tomorrow could be better than today, but deep down I can't forget yesterday though it already happened and passed.

What happens when you get tired of waiting for that person to do right and you move on? What do you do when you finally get tired of the bullshit get tired of pretending it's all good? I don't care too much if he's mad at me hell he should be mad at himself for the way he treated someone who cared for him. I don't care too much if we don't speak because now true feelings are coming out. The last words we spoke was when he called me and told me never to call again because he was mad that me and his sister were talking about him on facebook. Really he should feel like shit because all I did was post a status, not even directed too him. It's not my fault I was describing a jerk.

Tarun, I want to find it in my heart to hate him, I really do, but then again I put all this on me. I knew what I was getting myself into. It's a shame that the ones who swear they'd never hurt you are the ones that hurt you the most. There's some good in you, I see it I know there is but I couldn't bring out your full potential. So sad to see you caught up in this hood shit, when really it hasn't done anything for you, you put all your heat in soul in these streets to these niggas who care about you for the moment but yet you steady turn your back on those who bring out the best in you. He don't want me, he wants Kooda and I thought that was ok, but I still don't get how is it Kooda? The same Kooda he called a stalker, and said they aren't even like that, yea whatever you got caught up and now here you are on Facebook talking about you always wanted to be that girl's man. You little cock sucker, you think, I'm crazy you haven't seen nothing yet, psycho is the word best fit to describe me. It's such a shame how you did me wrong, and it wasn't even like I did something to you. I been sitting here dumbfounded, so confused trying to figure out where we went wrong. Was it something I did? Was it something I said? Was it something you heard? Was it something I'm missing?- Dondria It's like a joke that everyone else gets but me. I feel bad because you're a nice girl, but was I not nice of a girl? I didn't ask for you to comment on my status, nor did I ask to feel the way I feel, and never did I ask you to say you love me especially if I would have known we'd turn out like this. Karma is a bad bitch, and I hope she bites you in the ass, better yet the penis, I hope it hurts like hell. Maybe you'll learn to stop thinking with your dick and use your brain.

My Mr. 23, I talked to him for the first time in a year since August of 2009 and I didn't even cry because I was at peace, I was okay know that he was okay considering the conditions he was facing. It felt so good hearing his voice, I know my daddy gone be pissed when he see that extra 10$ on the phone bill this month but at the time it was worth it, and I'd do it again. It doesn't matter what he did in his past because I'm here only for the present and the future. I just want this all to be over for him to be home and back on track. He tells me that he's getting his life together that he reads. If your still locked up once I get this published I hope this is one book you'll read. You know about my past about who and what I was and you saw past that and I'm doing the same for you. All that matters to me is who your trying to be and who you want to become. I love you and miss you.

Jo'Von taught me to love that of what I can not see because though it might not be seen psychically with us spending time with one another but you cant deny the smiles that are on my face, I learned to love what I can not feel because its already touched my heart and is with me forever. To trust what seems impossible and unreasonable just because it doesn't make sense now don't mean it wont make sense later. I have faith and I believe in what other people doubt because what's understood don't need to be explained.

Bri Bri I still the apple of my eye and I thank God everyday that she's in my life. Though she's not in sight she's forever in my heart. She'll always be my reason for change. As of right now she's too young to understand any of what's going on it's just something's that are outta our hands.

S.E.X

Lust is easy. Love is hard don't confuse the two

A kiss is a kiss, a touch is a touch. After I'm finished you gone love me so much. Kiss me from my neck all the way down to my feet, I aint bragging but my sex game aint been beat. Up and down nice and slow, clothes all off now lets go. Good and fast make it last and don't ever stop, cuz what I'm gone show you might make your heart stop. Do me right do me good, if you can't I know another that could.

What sells? Sex sells, always has and always will. You can gain anyone's attention whenever some form sexuality is involved. Why does sex sell? Everyone wants to feel good and be pleased either from someone else or themselves. Some enjoy the moans and groans, the sweat and feeling of two bodies touching. Lots of people me included thrive on that feeling, and don't know what we'd be doing without it. I've had my share of niggas, I ain't even gone lie. I been out here dirty thuggin since I was bout twelve. I know the game and how it go, how one night stands are, and the I see you when I see you. I heard all those if I didn't have a girl I'd be with you. Or I wanna leave her but I just cant. I thought we had a good thing going, no feelings, no drama no strings attached.

I can't recall myself ever actually having a one night, one night stand. They always turn into months, even years, I knew that it was strictly sex and still found myself getting attached. I aint gone play myself like, I'm some gullible, clingy chick, who can't get a boyfriend. After all I been through I just wanted relations without the relationship. The people I found myself hooking up with, we hung out, talked on the phone, it wasn't one of those types of things where we only call each other for sex, when we were around each other no questions asked we already knew what was going to happen. I didn't have a problem with it, until later on, I was worth more than just to give it up. I wanted to be like the kinds of people I hated, people in commited, stable and happy relationships. I wanted to be booed up but never really found the time.

Once upon not long ago, I was a hoe. And im admitting it, wont take it back, cuz I did the shit. –MariahLynn

If me and a guy are chilling, im feeling him, he's feeling, me and we have a understanding that this is something we both wanna do. The only question in my mind are we going back to his place or mine. And if that makes me a hoe, im admitting it, cant take it back cuz I did the shit.

And sometimes til this day well maybe ten months prior I still stood behind that. If I wanna fuck, imma fuck. We can go back to my place, and after im done imma smoke a ciggerate and ask what are you about to do and that's my polite way of telling you to go so I can get back to the regular programing. Cuz if I went back to his place he would do the same thing. If I wanted to cuddle and what not I would get a hotel where im at least I paid for us to stay til the next morning or I would get me a boyfriend. I can fuck who I want, when I want, wanna know why? Cuz I motherfucking can! That's why. At the end of the day its my business. My bills are paid, my houschold is straight and my daughter was taken care of. Not saying that anybody else other than me is paying my bills, but if I want to do anything, I deserve it, cuz I do everything I am supposed to do. I don't know if my train of thought is all fucked up or what, but as a woman and a grown woman at that who's had sex just to do it, after a while its meaningless, its something you do because you have needs, and you keep it pushing.

Someone once told me you have options why not explore them? If the dude your with is fucking up, what do you do? Kick his ass to the curb and get you another one. And nobody would talk about you for that. Well what happens when you just have a long line of fuck ups? People start to question and think she just has bad taste in men, bad luck, her pussy attracts asswholes? And secretly people start to question your morals values and character.

Even Drake said "All those other men were practice, they were practice for me (for me for me). You don't know what you deserve until you've had it and anything else you have that isn't up to your expectations or what you read in those fairy tales or what you've seen growing up you go searching for it. And in my mind all I was doing was searching, even the bible says seek and you shall find. Knock and it shall be open unto you. Well I was just knocking on the wrong doors, I was seeking attention and after a while didn't care where I was coming from. After a while you get defeated by the loneliness, and you take whatever you can get.

Well I was the underdog, I stayed in the friendzone, then I glowed the fuck up and people started to notice. Got a lil ass, my own place, a car, started taking better care of myself and once I started to care, so did they. All in my inbox, liking everything I post on instagram and facebook, retweeting and favoriting my tweets. And watching my stories on snapchat 3 or 4 times.

One thing no nigga could ever say about me was that it was bad, and if they did they one lying mother fucker. I've been told that a couple times but in every case it was because I couldn't give into the temptation anymore, and I didn't find it exciting, I wanted to be more then just a friend, just a booty call, just a fling.

What is a fling?

Something, that you know doesn't have the potential to be anything more. Just a phase, a non serious relationship. A "fuck buddy" a friend with benefits. The question I wanted answered was if were just "friends' how many other friends does that person have. Sometimes I've been with people who were single, and sadly some who were in a relationship. I used to think, that a fling could turn into the real thing if you let it. There's no way in hell of that ever happening.

You know how there's always that one person that your not suppose to like but find yourself liking them anyway? I met Day Day through my old home girl Amanda, he used to be her dude way back when. She tells me how she still loves that boy and wants to marry him someday. When I first saw him I was like ewe, he not my type he were skinny jeans and got white boy swag and that ain't for me. It's something about tight jeans that turn me off. She did introduce me and once I started to get to know him I came to find out that he was really cool. Since he and Amanda weren't friends anymore and things weren't going well with us I found myself talking to Day Day all the time. We went walking around the development laughing and joking, my dad told me that I knew what I was doing wasn't right but how was I wrong? Was it wrong holding a conversation with a new friend even known it was my friends ex? It becomes a problem when the conversation becomes feelings. Feelings you cant control, when you try to fight a feeling it only gets stronger.

I never been the type of chick to take what don't belong to me or be fake especially when everybody loved me for my down to Earthiness. Walking down the hill I almost shit bricks and swallowed my tongue when I seen Amanda run outside. It felt so strange having her just down right stop and look at me with that blank stare of jealousy, and confusion. I kept telling Alex, my dad and everyone along with myself that I didn't like that boy. Everyday I found myself falling for his charm just a little bit. I could talk to Day Day for hours just laughing and joking and trust me when I tell you that sex never was a topic.

I cant say he was my best friend but he was a really good friend. Someone I could jus t sit up and talk to about whatever. It was obvious I had a crush on him but I knew it was wrong. Even if I did like him, I wasn't going to say anything. The littlest words could have the biggest impact on a friendship, or even a relationship. I kept my feelings to myself because getting to involved in something would be stupid and I didn't want to hurt Amanda's feelings because I knew how she felt even if he didn't feel the same.

Wednesday night my dad went to bible study and Day Day said he was coming over and I thought he was playing. About five minutes later he was calling telling me he was outside. When I opened the door I was in complete shock because I never really thought he was going to show. We flirted just a bit I took his keys and his hat. He told me that if I didn't give him back his hat or keys he was going to take my pants. I felt his hand on my thigh and I liked it. I should have stopped it but I didn't. He kissed me and I kissed him back, I wrapped my hand around his neck and held him as tight as I could. Every time I kissed him I could feel this tingle come over my body.

As much as I liked him, and was not just sexually attracted to him, he was just a fling, a phase, someone who was there when I needed him and I knew as fast as he was here, he could be gone. I was doing my thing and Day Day was doing his, and nomatter who we did our thing with, Wednesday was our thing. I don't care what we had planned, we made a way for one another. But at some point Wednesday was just another day, it has no meaning, no morals, no value.

It was this feeling I couldn't shake, couldn't let it go. In the back of my mind I knew what I was doing was wrong, but it just felt so right. I knew that even without sex Day Day was gone forever be my friend, but I just wanted to be friends, nothing more nothing less. I couldn't take the risk of getting caught and fucking up anymore, so what arose so fast, faded the same way.

Its all fun and games but what happens when feelings get involved someone's gonna get hurt. You're hoping and praying that, that someone isn't you. You do things you know are wrong but it just feels so right. You feel comfortable in his company and can talk too him about anything but in the end you still lose. Its a shame the things we do for a little affection. Friendships are broken and then comes the awkward silence when you too see one another. I never understood why is it, you can say you love me and call me too say hi when you want something, but when you see me in public you act as if we never met.

I let my emotions get the best of me a couple of times, but this time my mind was completely opposite of my emotions, mind and judgment. I met this boy Hampton, through a girl in my dorm. We were all out smoking drinking, and I thought to myself, aww he's so adorable. It got late and it was time for us to go back to the room and my girls had planned on them staying the night, but each of us would have had to sign someone in. my first instinct "I don't know this damn boy from Adam, and I'll be damned if he try some stupid stuff, I aint fuckin him" I had a lot of liquor in my system and we did have sex. Now I could use Jamie Foxx's excuse and blame it on the alcohol but in reality, I wanted too. It didn't make me no never mind because I thought it would be a one time thing, and I wasn't going to see him again. That didn't happen.

Hampton had been around for a while, everybody on my floor in my dorm knew who he was. I felt as if he lived there or something. Everyone kept asking do we go together and if not why don't we? "He's here all the time, we see this spark in your eye and how your always smiling when he's around, and when he leaves I get all depressed and lock myself in my room. Things were going beyond good, for the first time things actually felt great. There was no pressure, no commitment, no nothing, I didn't feel the need to rush into anything with him, we were friends, he was my best friend. My best friend who supplied the dro and the drank, and good laughs always talking bout some "you gone learn what a long dick look like today" Kevin Hart repeating ass.

I was pissy drunk, but what people don't know about me is that I am a very good listener. I couldn't help over here Hampton talking and I don't recall much, but the word "girlfriend" was stuck in my head everything else sounded like the teacher from Charlie brown *Wamp, Wamp, Wamp.* I thought that I was just hearing things and so instead of me confronting the issue right then and there, I waited till I sobered up too see if I could still remember it. I did. So when confronted about it there was only one answer given. "You didn't ask so I didn't tell" Now anybody in there right mind, would have left it alone, but I felt something for Hampton, I loved the fuck out of that boy, I loved that he would come up to Wayne State and visit me, and how he took me and Ran bowling. And he took me to go cash my paycheck. We had a not only good friendship but a great one, and I didn't mind that much that he had a girlfriend, just as much as I didn't mind laying next to him, rubbing his head or having him come up to Wayne State to visit me.

Now mind you, what I was doing was wrong, but he was even more wrong than I was, and if he didn't see anything wrong with it, neither did I. No offense, what did I have to lose, besides a friendship that I knew wasn't going anywhere? One day we were walking to the store and I felt that I just had to ask about his girlfriend, it was like she never even existed or he just never wanted to bring his girlfriend up to the girl he was screwing. But I felt I had the right to know, at least he owed me that much? He told me that they had been together almost two years. I couldn't help but think how could you throw something that valuable away? He made me understand that relationships aren't as simple as people try and portray them. Even though you have ups and downs and they can work your last nerves and though at times you feel like giving up and walking out, you still try. You don't ever just give up one the person that you love even if at times you hate them. I could tell he loved her, and I knew that what I felt wasn't half that. I accepted the fact that even though he was my bestfriend, that's all he was. In every relationship there's one girl one guy, one ex still trying, one hoe that tries to interfere, and one friend secretly hoping it ends. And secretly I was that friend.

Having sex isn't just a psychical; it's an emotional and mental thing. You're nothing more than just a piece of ass. You begin to wonder do they have feelings. Sex doesn't make your problems go away, whoever told you that was a bald faced liar. It only creates them, you hear the rumors on things you know damn well didn't happen. It ruins friendships you lose friends that way and find out who got your back. Sex isn't my friend, we don't look at things the same way. Why is it boys can have sex with any bitch they please and not get talked about?

I rather be stuck up with my cookies their mine so why not. I ain't bout to just pass em out like it's some kind of donation. I'm not trying to feed these niggas. You see them girls that let everybody ride her jus like a bus route and I refuse to let that be me. I haven't met a female yet that has meant to get a name for themselves. Three turns into seven, then that triples and you add eight more. I've been told that I look like a bad bitch from behind and that I got a great future behind me. Some boys just can't keep there thoughts in their head they have to tell me. They tell me what they game do, how they gone do me and my body some good that they would be the best I ever had. Like I haven't heard it all before. I feel I'm addicted to sex, I want it need it and just got to have it. I'd go crazy without it because my body fens for it.

Sucking dick is something that 9 out of 10 females I met said they would never in their life do. When really 2 out of those 9 say they don't know if they would, they cant say. 1 out of that 10 everybody knows sucks dick and is never involved in the conversation. Then you secretly have about 3 of those people who have thought about it and at least one that will admit to wanting to just to try it or just on that right person. So most of the bitches that say they don't or wont suck dick are lying. Now me, I can't say that I would or I wouldn't I'm undecided. Personally I don't think it's wrong I just think it's wrong when the female is stupid and sucks a nigga up when she needs to look at it as a favor for a favor. It's wrong when a girl just puts her lips on any and just about every nigga dick and thinks nothing of it.

People ask me all the times about one night stands, I've been there done that and a lot of the times I never looked back at them. Do I approve? Personally myself I used to think you only live once but that's kind of logic breaks up relationships, holds STD's and brings babies into this world. So as for me no I do not approve but you can do whatever the hell you want to. Sex changes everything, the way you feel about people, how you look at them, that's when your true feelings come out.

It seems that sex has always been an uncomfortable topic for me to talk to any one about. I held back details because my sex life was just that my sex life. What I did in the privacy of whoever's home was my personal business and should not be discussed. I don't want to be anyone's laughter, and for them to know how I am in bed. It's just you should be in a stable relationship and have complete trust. I say that at least most of the people I had sex with were a boyfriend one time or another. Then the rest of them were just one night stands that stayed around so I guess you can call them booty calls.

Men are tricky, they just cant make up their minds. They want a good girl but they turn around and leave her for the wild one who's down for the fun. And when a man has that girl who just gives it up whenever he goes off to be with the sweet girl is I willing to wait.

It's crazy because a boy can fuck every girl A-Z but when I meet a Tom Dick or Harry I get called a whore, and you be wondering what im doing and who im with. Your connected to everyone you've had sex with and tied to everyone that he's had sex with. I want you to like me to be able to say she wasn't some girl I was bangin we real cool, but sadly that's all we are just sum jawn you hit way back when. If you call a boy and aint talken bout sex he quick to say he busy.

Remember when I told you I come from a place where sex was scared? What happens when the meaning is gone? What happens when sex becomes more like a hobby or sport to see who can win MVP? When sex becomes an adjective, has no objective, no reason that's when you know it's gotten too far. Sex needs to get its rightful title back. I look at is as anybody can have sex, but it takes time, effort, compassion and trust to make love.

Steve Harvey said something about having a 90 day rule. And now that I think about it, it makes perfect sense now. The 90 day rule gives you time to see where his or her mind is at. To get to know them and see what your about to get yourself into. See if they are really into you or just really into having sex with you. When you jump into sex and then try to establish a relationship sex is all it becomes. Let that someone prove to you that he deserves not only your body, let him earn your trust and respect.

I have a prime example of someone who was just the opposite, the one thing I did love about him was he did not believe in sugarcoating anything, and I mean anything. I got his number on a Sunday and the very next day, he was already texting me telling me he wanted to fuck. That is an immediate turn off, I think it's disrespectful. I had met up with him on Friday and all he could about was taking me into the bathroom, and wanting to come up to my room and do all of these things to me. As creepy as he was, he was two times as fine, and in the back of my mind I wondered why was he so sexually attracted to me? He to me I was hot and I just thought it was because I had some ass. I didn't care to know what the real reason was, I didn't have the time. He only texts me to ask can he come over, and that he misses me, and I'm like nigga! You don't even know me.

SEX, don't think I'm saying that you shouldn't have it or shouldn't do it. I just want to make sure that if you have it it's with the right person for the right reasons. Everybody looks at if differently. Some think because they are in a relationship they have to have it. Now mind you I've had my fair share and a lot of them I wish I could take back because they weren't with the right people and some were for the wrong reasons. I've had sex to get back at people, to get my own self-satisfaction. I've had it because I not only thought it was what he wanted I thought I wanted it as well.

Parents need to be more open minded and willing to talk about sex. I mean just because I ask about sex don't assume that I'm having it. I just want to be prepared and know what to do when I come across that bump in the road. You need to break it down and not with those old birds and the bees. Tell me what most guys are thinking, what they look for, what they want and tell me how they go about getting it. Tell me that look you may think it's the best think and that it will solve all my problems it isn't going to change anything. Nine times outta ten it only makes it worse. If your doubting sex or cant find a reason to have it chances are sex isn't for you.

𝓕riends

I'd rather have an enemy who admits they hate me, instead of a
friend who secretly put me down

No Privacy

Those who laugh and gossip with you! Will laugh at your expense and gossip about you. You can tell lot about a person just by their choice of friends. If your friends are loud, full of drama, chaotic liars, people will think you are an instigator. Our friends describe who we are, what we accept and are willing to deal and put up with. I don't know what there is to say about me. My friends are all of thee above. Loud, Daring, Assholes, Head busters, Ride or Dies, Confusing, Sneaky, and a bunch of bitches but I wouldn't change them for anything. I'm so surprised that through it all, they have stood by me, supported me, and loved me. For people to be my friend the way I meet you is the way I expect you to stay. I come off a little strong and a bit strange but that's just how I am. I don't sugar coat shit if you don't like it you just won't. I've always been that friend that no matter what when you need me I'll be there.

Friends are important. FRIENDSHIP: It is the only ship that never sinks, though at times you wanna throw them over board. I realized that a true friend grows stronger threw any obstacle thrown their way. A pretend friend fades away and don't value the friendship and it doesn't matter if you leave or stay. At the end of the day I know that my friends and I will argue and disagree but it's those things that bring us closer. If we can't laugh at our past there is no future. Just about every friend I've had we have gotten into it some worse than others. That just shows me that they can deal with my bullshit.

I've been a sneaky little backstabber, we have all been there at some point. I can't just say I'm one of the realest bitches you know, I hate when people do that I hate fake people pretending to be real. People lie everyday about the simplest shit. I lie about not eating the last cookie, or who drunk the last of the kool-aid. I might not tell a story the exact way it was told to me, it happens and sometimes it's never on purpose. You can quote me a thousand times and still say it wrong. If it didn't come out my mouth I didn't say it. If people lie to God each and everyday in their prayers, in their promises and in their actions what makes you think they won't lie to you?? One thing that Rhonda told me that I'll always apply now, "Dont tell mfs yo bussiness, if u really have to let it out the only one u better tell is God. God's the only one who won't judge you, or run back and tell."

Why do we hold on to that friend that we know isn't such a good influence? Sometimes that friend is the one you connect with, and are closet with. There is something about all of my friends that I love, I bond and can talk to them about anything. My parents say I choose the most undesirable people to be my friends. I know right from wrong, and I can make my own choices. I cant change them, and want to learn from this if it is a mistake.

I had just gotten my paycheck from my place of work, and as we walked out the door the bus rode past us. We ran up this hill full of snow thinking we could catch it on its way to the station. As we climbed up the hill Tay lost her shoe in the depths of the snow. She over reacted about the whole thing, instead of bitching and complaining she could have been getting her shoe. We finally got up the hill and missed the bus. We went back down the hill and again Tay lost her shoe. She fell on me and we were both soaked when we got up. I had seen the bus in a far distance so I drug her until we made it to the bus stop.

We get to the mall and just buy everything that we could just about fit. We got to Steve N Berry's with no intention of stealing, but wound up doing it anyway. Getting the clothes without being spotted was the hardest part we thought, because we didn't know if they had undercover security or not, but walking out the store was even harder than we thought. Not once did we hear any type of detection button go off when the man stopped us. Tears fall from Tay's eyes as soon as he touches her.

He told us to give him our information, if no parent could come and get us we would be going to juvenile. As we fill out the paper I already spotted that everything Tay wrote down wasn't true at all. From just that I knew I would have to be the one who got us out of this mess as always. I had the man call my grandma Cookie to come and get us. My grandma was more amused than mad, she just couldn't believe that I was stealing. Now Tay was a different story because she's not her grandkid.

They finally got a hold of her real information sending the both of us a letter saying we had to appear in court and pay the money back. I wasn't going to pay and neither was Tay. We already established our stories and that nothing would happen. I had seen Tay in a couple of weeks, until we went into the court house. For some reason this didn't bother Tay that we might be going to jail. Tay told her story first, I couldn't believe what was coming out her mouth. She was making it out to be as if I planned on stealing that she knew it was wrong and went along with tit anyway.

The moment we walked out that court room I lost all respect for Tay. I wanted to kick her ass, because she tried to put the blame on me. I wonder if I got the chance to speak first what I would have said? I might have done the same thing but at least made it seem like I did have some part in it. I didn't make her do anything, if she wanted to join she could. It wasn't like I put a gun to her head, she was a willing co-accomplice.

So I told my story, I'm not one to blame anyone for the decisions I make. If I wanted to leave I could have but I didn't, something wouldn't let me because I wanted something as well. It's so funny because now Tay and I can look back at that day and just laugh.

Tay and I have the craziest, weirdest friendship, but we understand eachother, and even with all the bad that we've been through, the running up curbs hitting cars, going on flights it's the most fun I've ever had. Sometimes I question that damn girl, I feel like she's my sister. We can tell eachother anything. There were times I wondered how the hell did our friendship last this long? But who cares how and why all that matters is that it did.

Like with A.B at first I wanted to bash the shit out of her, and tell how much I hated her, but that's not even me. I think she's a sweet girl, somewhere, and I tried my best to bring that out of her. I learned that you can't change, fix or help everyone, they have to want it on their own. Even though she got me jumped, and I had to go to court I reached out to her on twitter. I wanted her to know that there's no longer any bad blood. But it took a lot for me to come to that conclusion because I promised myself that I was gone kick her ass whenever I went back to jersey. I held a grudge long enough, and Im a lot older, and holding a grudge doesn't do anything. And I am glad I reached out to her.

The one thing I did hate about her besides her bi-polar attitude was that she surrounded herself with the wrong crowd, and she went about relationships all wrong, and I knew first hand what road she was going to end up at. I know what it feels like to just want to be loved, and that sometimes when you want something so bad, you'll do whatever it takes at any cost to get it.

If I could say anything to A.B it would be that when you look for love in all the wrong places it will find you and break your heart, break it into a million pieces and wont look back. Everybody who smiles in your face aint your friend and you need to realize who your real friends are in the first place. Don't be so willing to let everyone in your life because people will come in and they will do their best to make and watch you fail. You have to put your heart as well as your mind in the right place because that determines whats gonna happen in your life.

I wish her the best, and I do miss you at times, because we did have some unforgettable moments, and though we made a lot of bad decisions and mistakes, those are what makes us who we are.

"Ericka I need you in my life, you have no idea how glad I am I met you. Wit you I feel safe, you like the only girl that's been through what I've been through and knows how I'm feelin. I can be honest wit

you, you are a real friend. I always got ya back you have a shoulder to cry on and a cracker to get wild with. Times are hard and wiggas {whites and niggas} are mean. I can tell you anything, I can trust ya silly ass."
Love Alex

Alex you have no idea how glad I am that I've met you. There's just times when I need someone jut to listen and feel what I feel. I'm glad that you have a car and we jus go riding to get the fuck away from everybody's bullshit. I have no concerns about your past. You past is were it should be behind you and that's where it needs to stay. I don't care what anybody says about you even if it's true because who cares. I'm so glad your in my life. I met you October 15th, 2009 at exactly 12:47pm it was on a Thursday. We've had so many good times since then and I couldn't ask for a better friend. I love you so much and thank God everyday that he has placed you in my life because you mean and do a lot for me. I feel as if I never tell you thank you enough. Alex you know when I'm not my normal self and the days when I just need a hug. Your a little rowdy and honestly I never thought we'd be as close as we are today.

As for my other best friend Emoni, my little chocolate chip she's so sweet but has a bad side to her and she makes me giggle. Shes the one who says you know that isn't right but when you do it I'll be standing there right beside you. Your never in any kind of non sense and that's what I love about you. I wouldn't change the way you are not for no amount of money in the world. The Summer of 2010 me and Emoni grew really close and I can say I love Emoni to death because she's there for me, she always keeps it real with me and know how to manage her friends and her boyfriend.

To Alex and Emoni

Though we act a bunch of lesbo's on a daily basis we don't always act like total assholes. We do have real serious moment that we come across in our lives. I've never been one to cry and there's days when I sit in her car and cry my ass off like a baby. I love you two and I cant even find the words to say how glad I am to have you as my bestfreinds.

True friends are really hard to come across Alex and Emoni are always there for me and I'm so fucken glad that you have come into my life. Some people are just meant to be in your life and you two are those people. It's like were three of a kind, were the three best friends that anyone can have. I can relate to you guys. When you don't have someone who's there when you need them most, to be there picking your noise holding your hand, driving you around or just loving you when your least deserving of it cuz that's when you need it most life would be hard.

Then there are sometimes when even the best of friends have yet to see brighter days. Like with me and Alex. Alex has a boyfriend Mack, and I think he world of him because he makes my bestfriend happy but I felt I had to compete with Mack to spend time with Alex. So deep down I became a little jealous because I was there before Mack and I don't want to say that he was stealing her from me but he was stealing the time that I spent with her. We began to argue over little petty stuff and that bothered me more than anything because that wasn't the friendship I knew.

Please do not reply to wat im writting i dont want to start a facebook war... im really gonna try to be civil.. i feel like over the last few months ive always tryed to help you in anyway and you saying i was a bad friend really hurt my feelings... i know im not the best.. but wat got me is how you pointed out wat i DID wrong.. that i dont listin or i dont ask... or that i dont spend time with you... i understand that things changed wen i started dating Mack..it all started wen i invited him to the ac trip...thats wen emoni started her attitudes with me & u starting feeling like im chosing him over you.. i dont know wat to say but thats my bf & u were my friend i didnt wana be in the position to choose over any of you but its obvious this is not working.. the attitude you had towards me & mine back to you... all it is, is awkward car rides & phone calls. When i was with you i always felt free to be myself(unlike i was with emoni) i knew i wasnt being judged bcuz you been threw .the same things.. i felt like you were my soul mate... that i could tell you anything and we could lean on eachother threw it all .. we could make eachother laugh but in our hearts know eachothers pain & want to party it out... things surely did change once u came home from Michigan & im sorry i didnt ask you about the emotional promblems but i did listen to everything you told me ... but lately as i did bring up about a month ago i could sense this attitude you constantly had towards me & i felt like i was being a bother to you (thats why i didnt wana go on walmart or mall trips) and with Emoni.I dont know wat to say bout that ! i can tell she doesnt wana be friends by the lil status she put up tonight & the snippy things she says threw txt...so be it! nothing anyone can say will get threew to her were both stubborn so as much as it hurts to say i guess BUBBLES & GIGGLES is nomore. Yes, i was very hurt thats why i deleted you both.. i didnt feel like lookin at ether of u no offense... it really started that day at work wen you told me you guys planned an ac trip on a saturday..(i know it wasnt on purpose but you both knew i work at the hospital

EVERY saturday) so that hurt me alot & i just felt horrible & pissed & very upset cuz you guys planned a big trip like that without me... then sleepovers & more sleepovers then today i see underneth your picture on your page were it used to say my name on both ya pages i was replaced & i felt disconnected & kinda thrown out of our friendship &

Ericka ; Shelley ; Lola ; etc.*♥*) and i wasn't even in that group i just felt kicked out & it really hurt to think my two best friends aren't my friends no more & it really sucks to lose you both... but i guess things like this just happen Ericka: Sorry but i feel as if i have to respond because this is a better way instead of arguing. 1} The Ac trip, like i told you it never bothered me that Mack was going because i think he's awesome and I'm glad you two are happy and if he makes you happy then I'm happy i rather listen too the good then the bad with Aaron n Justin 2} Yes there are times i feel as if you choose Mack over me, i understand you work and such and wanna spend time with him but the moment you start lying to me i feel very hurt and disrespected because i thought we were honest, and i never wanted you too feel you had to choose between us, because you shouldn't have too that's why i invited James to bowling night because i knew deep down that's what Emoni wanted and i wanted too make her happy even though it want a very good idea. 3} The attitude i have with you was never on purpose it was just i didn't know how to get through to you because its clear to me when you don't like or agree with something you want to hang up and not listen as if it doesn't matter. So my question too you is does this friendship matter, is all the time and car rides and tears and laughs and jokes and holding hands worth losing over the fact that non of us want to be wrong and that we are hurt. I always felt close too you because yes you and i were more alike we see eye too eye on most things and i valued that about our friendship it meant the world too me that i had someone who understands me who i can be real with. 4} when i came back from Michigan yes i was hurt, hell i was broken i felt alone because the people i loved moved on and it's so hard too talk about because you know how i fell about Edrick and its so hard to bee in a long distance relationship. to want someone who doesn't want you, to want what you cant have, I thought everything was gone be ok but it wasn't, the love of my life wasn't in love with me anymore, my niece might not know how i am and that kills me, i was depressed i gained weight and it took everything i had too smile and act as if i was ok, im not one too cry or show how i feel but last night got too me because this friendship meant something and its not worth losing. 5} i cant speak upon you and Emoni but i dont want too be the reason bubbles and giggles is no more because b4 i came along you too were happy so im sorry if i came between you too 6} i feel like deleting me was so stupid, it was childish, i feel like this before your facebook said Ericka n Emoni i love you too, then it changed too that rawr means i love you in dinosaur how do you think i felt to be replaced by that stuff, so since you took me off i took you off then Emoni put me up so i put her up. if you felt kicked out it was because you never made time for us anymore, and we all played a part in this and yes I'm sorry for saying it started with you but i feel as if it did, when Mack wasn't around i was ur go to girl, you were always at my house then when he came along i couldn't get too minutes of your time so i made other friends beside you. and when i made other friends you just spent more time with Mack I understand you work and want to be with Mack but what about me? do i not matter anymore.?? 7} And no our Ac trip wasn't on purpose but Saturday was the only good day for anybody. When you want too do something you have no problem taking off work at the hospital so don't feed me that b.s talken bout your hurt, because your not the only one who's hurt so stop saying your hurt because I'm hurt too but it seems like nobody's feelings matter but yours. As far as the sleepovers, you are never available and i feel as if i have to make an appointment to hang out with you, I do try to hold on too this friendship i do try and invite you over but you lied you should have told me the truth instead lying too me, if u would have told me then i wouldn't have been mad i would have wanted you too come over and we work this out 8}sometimes there are things just out of our hands and I'm guessing this time is one of those things we cant control. I'm sorry you fell this way but you not the only one that's hurting so please keep that in mind. I am really sorry you feel like that, but its life and we all have hard times but the thing about it is how we look at it and I'm guessing none of us look at it in a good way.

Me and Alex's friendship was never the same, we did try for a while, but it was fading, and fading fast. We haven't spoken much, I reached out to her when my dad told me she was getting married, and in the back of my mind that pissed me off even more. Because I was there for her n Macks whole relationship and for her to tell my dad and not me about their marriage hurt. We had talked a couple times since then, and on New Years of 2012 she text me, and told me how the New Years of 2010 we vowed that, that was going to be our best year. I have to admit it was, because it was the year I spent with all four of my girls, Alex, Emoni and even Amanda. But it was 2011 that we didn't make that vow and that's when all hell broke lose truthfully. There are times when I miss the friendship we had, and I do wish her the best and im glad she's happy and I still do love my little snow bunny.

Then I have Erica my twin. I trust her with all that I have, she's always been there with the best advice keeping my head on solid ground. I had known her since my days of Birch Park when I was a young dummy. Before I knew all the things that I know now, she was there when this good girl went bad. Erica knows everything that there is to know about me. I know that she has my best interest at heart because she never gave up on me even when I gave up on myself. I never told her how thankful I am that she's stood by me when I was too weak to stand for myself.

Toe Toe, my first bmoms, I love her to death, she kept it 100 with me since day one. I told her once and never had to tell her again, I'd kill a bitch for her and I meant it. It was a while back when she was , I went on the West side and showed my ass, I knew she could hold her own, but I had to think about Ray, he was innocent and couldn't defend himself. I took a hammer threw it through the window, and had a Jasmine Sullivan moment. At first I felt bad because I would never want for someone to do such horrible acts to my home nor car, but I ride for mines. Never once did I have a care in the world about going to jail, and I know that sounds so ignorant, but hey we have our moments.

I have Stasha, we've been through so much, and yet, we sit back blow one in the air and reminisce on the past. Stasha was always my partner in crime, my ace boon coon. I remember I met her at church, she was such a sweet girl, but she had an evil side I tell you that. We went around town causing trouble, as my mom would say Dumb and Dumber wreaking havoc on society, till this day, I wonder who was dumb and who was dumber. I feel like she was like my long lost sister and we were making up for lost times, or we were Siamese twins, conjoined at the hip.

Cant forget, my last babymomma DeErris, my bestie, when I first met her I didn't think we would be friends. That bitch was loud, crazy and wild, just like me, and having to much in common I felt we were bound to bump heads. That was not the case at all. I love her to pieces she's the devil on my shoulder, telling me you only live once so make every moment count.

No Privacy

I have Meech, Metra and Mauree, through thick and thin we will always be friends. Distance will never bring us apart. Friends who I love and miss so much. We've had our bumps in to road but we held on strong and jumped over them shits. I don't know if they remember when we went to Webber, and when it was the "it thing" to talk shit in the text books. We wrote our names everywhere. "MnMs I'll never forget it. Those were the days, but those days got us in a lot of trouble and made a lot of people mad. Got so deep that we even fell out, but we fell back together, as we should have.

I cant forget about my crazy ass ten stars. When I say them my bitches, I say that with the most respect. I love them broads, at though we don't speak or talk as much as we used to since I moved. We have been through so much, and at the end of the day we have always rode for one another and that's never gonna change.

The beautiful thing about friendship, is that when you feel like giving up, there's this voice in the back of your mind, you see this projectile image of all the good and it outweighs the bad.

Some days I don't care if I don't have friends, shit that's less drama for me. I roll solo dolo those are just less people birthdays I have to remember. I don't have to get them nothing, deal with there mess or waist no money. I look at it this way aint nobody truthful, so I don't have to listen to your lies. I stay to myself I'm not saying I don't want to have friends, because I have a couple and I don't even label them as friends but family. To me you either have associates, people you label as family or nothing. I don't do the whole frienemies thing, if I don't trust you I'm not going to deal with you. Bitches smile in my face all the time. They act as if I don't know they be slick dissin me on the low. You know what I do, some days I feed into it because I know I got what they want. Other days I distance myself until I'm completely gone because I don't wanna hurt their feelings.

Sometimes I could careless about another hoe and they lifestyle. If you don't contribute anything to me your useless, I don't mean to sound mean and heartless but that how life is. I'm just stating the facts and telling you how it's going to be done. I don't mean to sound like a total bitch because I'm not, I just ain't down to tolerate nonsense. If your not with me your against me. We all look at friends differently. It doesn't matter if you like them, or don't have them they exist. Let me be the one to tell you if you have a friend that's always in drama and for some reason you get dragged in it let them go. I know you don't wanna leave them alone, but worry about you, and your safety. Or you have that friend who is always doing wrong? At first it might be just based on fun, then you may not know how to tell them that's enough.

I mess with these bitches sideways cause aint none of these hoes straight. Even though you and your friend may be close you should never tell them all your deep dark personal business. Something's you keep to yourself. I don't' care how close you two are, nine times outta ten what you told them has come up. Either unintentional or on purpose because they are mad and want to get you back. I put my trust in one to many bitches, but I didn't learn my lesson. I continued to be so open hearted and wondered why my name was in so many people mouths? When you put all of your confidence and let your guard down once you get into all those secrets get exposed. Because some girls are nothing more than dirty ass bitches who would kill to see you fall and unhappy. They see yo man and take him, not because they like him because they want what you have.

A good friend is honest there is never any reason to lie. Though they might not give you a life story they tell as much about them as they want you to know as well as remember. We tell it like it is no sugar coating nothing, for what? As long as you are trying to help them and not hurt them they will listen at times they my not want to hear it. A good friend is fun unique and over the top and always interesting. You have your take on fun. Some friends are fun because they are the life of the party and always give you something to do. Challenge you wanting you to see everything while they can. Some notice the little things about you.

A good friend is a good listener can tell whenever you are upset and can read your mind. supportive and loyal you never worry if they have your back or not. They are trustworthy you can leave them in a room and know they wont steal anything. You know they wont steal ya man and then bad talk you. They wont damage your reputation. They don't gossip or dickeat. Good friends make it known when they care about you. Sticks with you not only thought he good but as well as the bad.

Most all of all a good friend isn't judgmental they accept you for who you are even when you are acting like a bitch. They are patient and help you learn from your mistakes. They forgive you even when your wrong.

I had a friend like that his name was Day Day. He was someone I could always depend on. Who was a shoulder to cry on, never judged me and was a great listener. He knew all my deepest darkest secrets and I trusted him with them all. He never gossiped and wasn't in drama. He stayed at home but always made time for me. The only flaw about Day

Day was that he was my stuffed animal. When the world felt like it was turning its back on me Day Day was always there. Day Day was my backbone, my support, my everything. He was everything I wanted and everything I needed. Good friends are the ones you don't have to ask anything of, they just know and can make your whole day brighter.

Lessons in Friendship
1. Be Yourself

It may seem like a no-brainer, but a lot of teens struggle not to lose their identity once they become part of a group of friends. Though who you are is always changing, especially during your teenage years, some aspects of your personality will stay pretty much the same. Figure out what those things are and think hard about who you want to be, then present yourself honestly and genuinely to the people you hang around with. Sometimes you're going to disagree or not be the most popular member of the group. However, you will always feel you've been true to yourself -- and that you haven't become somebody else's clone.

2. Avoid Gossip

Friends don't spread rumors about other friends -- even within their own group. If you've heard something shocking about someone you're friends with, find a considerate way of asking them about it personally. If you're not sure how to talk to them about it, seek the advice of one other trusted friend, but don't let the discussion turn into a free-for-all about everything you don't like about the person. You certainly wouldn't be happy if someone did that to you, so set a good example for others -- and for yourself. When you're mad at them don't start talking badly upon them because it will come back and the things you know can make or break them

3. Defend Your Friends

At some point, somebody you're not tight with is going to question the integrity of one of your friends. It's important to find out both sides of the story in a situation like this, but it's also a good chance to show your friend that you have faith in them by standing up for their reputation. Whenever you can, be respectful of the other person's question or criticism but emphasize that your friend is a good person who deserves the respect of others, even when they make mistakes.

4. Protect Your Friends
When a friend of yours is making not-so-great decisions -- whether it's about drugs, alcohol, studying or dating -- do your best to look out for them. This doesn't mean telling them what to do constantly, but you can offer gentle advice and guidance from time to time.If you give advice in a caring way that shows you value your friend and respect their feelings and wishes, they're much more likely to pay attention. Chances are, what you think means a lot to them, and you can be a good influence.

5. Be Careful About Boyfriends and Girlfriends
It's a good rule of thumb to stray away from dating the exes of your friends. It's an even better rule of thumb to avoid dating the people your friends have crushes on -- or people who have turned down your friends for dates. Even if your friend gives you the go-ahead, wait a while to get involved with someone who broke their heart or betrayed their confidence.

6. Return the Favor
There are times when a friend will lend you a jacket, a textbook or a shoulder to cry on. A good friend will pick you up when you're stuck in a rainstorm and listen patiently when you share a problem with them. Be sure that you're equally as generous with your time, your emotions and your possessions. People will take notice, and it's something to feel good about.

Lost No More

Father,
Broken dreams and shattered glass. The things you want never seem to last. Broken promises down the hall I'm walking on air and I'm still afraid to fall. Looking in the mirror I cant see my own reflection, all I see is lies, tears and rejection. If you can hear my why are you letting me cry? Why are you letting me down? Hath thou left and forsaken thy child? I feel so alone and by myself. I've been running for too long and I can't run any more. I'm tired and I was running from someone I could not escape, myself. It's time I face my problems, I'm afraid of having to go through this alone. I've been doing this for to long without anyone's help and haven't gotten the results I wanted. I surrender and am giving myself to you so you can help me. I am trying to give up my childish ways and mature into the young lady I was meant to be.

No Privacy

Have you ever seen the movie "Forrest Gump"? If so you remember Jenny the only friend Forrest had. Jenny was a lost soul who couldn't find herself in this cold hearted world. I feel that way sometimes, like I'm useless, pointless, meaningless, and worthless. There were days when I thought it would be better to end it, end the drama, the rumors, the lies, confusion and just plain bullshit in my life. My household was broken back in 2001 when my mom left my dad, he couldn't get over it and neither could I. I left the only family even though my brothers and sisters were a strained. When we left I didn't cry, I just watched my sister ball her eyes out. She cried the tears I refused too, I saw my mother get emotional. I thought me of all people would. I was the closet to my dad, I was a spitting imagine.

I didn't know what was going on, I was too young to understand any of it. I didn't know that morning before I went to school would be the last time I ever saw my father within a five year span. I acted out in school, not just because trouble wanted to meet me but I was crying out for attention. I built this hard shell that I wouldn't let anyone break. Everyone I let in hurt me so I promised to never do it again.

There are still times when no matter the house I'm in I know it will never be a home, and if it is a home it won't ever be my home. The last home I remember was when I was nine, when I had a mother and a father who I never would have thought would fall out of love with one another. When not only did I have one sister but four and two brothers with no prefix to separate us and dividing us as step. I walk down the hallways in the house looking for what was missing; I never knew it was my soul. On the inside I was dark, cold and bitter but I tried to hide it and above the surface I acted as if it was ok. I was angry because the life that I had known wasn't the same and was never going to ever be the same. I never knew that I would have to try to smile a real smile.

It's never ok to pretend that everything's going to be alright when you know its not. You can't keep fooling yourself, even if you're fooling others. You have to deal with what's going on and fix it. So I dealt with what was going on in my own way. I did drugs to distance myself to escape from reality and be placed outside the life I was living. I drank because I wanted to drown in my own sorrow and I had sex because deep down all I wanted was love. I was never peer pressured, didn't follow the crowd I did these things out of my own free will.

I was depressed, feeling all alone in the dark with nowhere to turn and nobody to turn too. It seemed everyone saw me but nobody was ever really paying attention. I was just a face that you couldn't remember, and a name you hardly ever could recall. I stayed in something, except in tune with myself. Have you ever looked in the mirror and didn't know what or who you were seeing. I saw my reflection but I couldn't see into my soul. I didn't recognize my on face. I tried to fight my problems without anyone's help, selfishly enough I would always fail. I was too ashamed to swallow my pride and ask for help. At times I wanted to just end all of my problems even if that meant ending the source of it all. My life seemed pointless and worthless, just a waist of time. I tried everything I could to drinking, smoking, took pills, choke, drown and one time suffocate myself. Nobody not even I really could tell you why I did it, all I can say it that it came a point when I just felt hopeless.

5;55

It was one of the darkest times in my life, when I was afraid, lost, and confused. When I left Michigan it was 5:55 everyday for months, when things got rough with my mom, no matter the time it was it always felt like 5:55 to me. I would lie in bed thinking things just couldn't get better. 5:55 reminds me of a place that I never want to be brought back too, a place that though I want to forget I never can. When I look out the window I can't see anything not even my reflection. I can't see past the darkness not even into my soul. Yes it's dark right now but it won't be dark forever. I see the sunset in the distance and that's what keeps me going, that is my faith, my hope and strive. That it may not be the best now but I have it easy, I have it good and 5:55 wont last forever.

I know there will be many times of 5:55 in my life it happens everyday, day in and day out. As long as I see the sun peeking out through the shadows I know there's light at the end of the tunnel.

After all that I was going through with my family, friends, and Edrick I just wanted to be by myself. I was an emotional wreck on several occasions for feeling so stupid. I went to the medicine cabinet took a pain pill, Tylenol, Advil, and bupropion some sleeping pills and wine cooler. That was sure too end it. I couldn't help but ask God to forgive me. I know this isn't my plan, I shouldn't give up. Why should I feel stupid things like this is human nature. God please don't hate me, I only want to be loved right now and if I don't have your love I have nothing at all. I was slowly drifting to sleep but not fast enough. I grabbed a scarf and choked the hell out myself. I felt my eyes trying to pop out the socket and that was too painful. Other times I had cut my arms, as I watched the blood drip and drop something wouldn't let me finish.

She's the greatest gift given and if it wasn't for her I couldn't tell you where I'd be. She's my inspiration, for motivation to dedication, she means everything. My light, my sunshine on a cloudy day, the reason why I smile and strive for success. Bri Bri's the rock that keeps me grounded, my hope my dream, my joy and goals. Bri Bri is my 5:56 in life and every minute after that.

When you have someone that changes your life for the better you know they were always meant to be there no matter how late in the game they came. I feel Briea came into my life right on time. I was on the wrong path and nothing could slow me down. When you have someone that even though you have plans you rather spend your time with them that's when you know their special. When you look at them you see yourself in their eyes, you can't imagine what your life would be without them. Do you have someone that you're not ashamed to love? That you'd do anything for?

From the very first moment I knew about you came into this world I told myself I would do better. When I first held you I knew you would be the reason I would want to change. You brighten my day and ease my pain. Whenever I hold you I feel like my life finally has its sense of completion. At times I might not be able to be there when you want me too, but I'll always be there when you need me. You're the perfect blessing that continues to bless me every single day. I don't know and can't imagine my life without you. You bring me so much joy and now I can smile and not think twice if it's real or not. I wonder what had my life had been if you were hear just a year or so before. No matter the time it would always be right. When you grow up, you may or may not think of me as one of your heroes, but you'll always be my hero. The one I look up too and make sure that I'm on the right track for.

For some the most influential in their lifetime would be their mother or father, someone who has lived their life and is very wise and gives good advice, but for me the most influential person hasn't even reached the age of four. My niece is big biggest inspiration, she is my reason for wanting to improve and succeed in life. I already wanted to attend college for myself, but when my niece was born I knew I had someone to strive for. I promised myself that not only would I tell my niece anything's possible but be a prime example that anything's possible. I want to be a respectable and positive role model. I believe everyone has someone to look up too, someone who gets them through the rough times in their lives.

10-14

Today I smiled a real smile and when I cried they were tears of joy. I never knew how beautiful life was until you came along. I cried because I was happy, and I finally felt complete, because on this day I met the greatest person I would ever meet. Her cry wasn't any cry it was a sign to let me know that I would always be there and never let her go. I never thought I'd see this day when all my hatred could be wiped away. She never spoke a word but it just always seemed right and as of 10-14 you changed my life.

NEVER say NEVER because you NEVER know what your capable of if you NEVER try. If I had to say never about anything it would be I NEVER knew I was capable of ever being able to forgive. FORGIVENESS is not what we do for other people, we do it for ourselves to get well and move on. I never knew that I was able to forgive those who hurt me, I never knew that being angry was only hurting me.

On the days I have bad days I think about the movie "Precious" "That was yesterday fuck that day, that's why God created new days". Not to dwell on the past but in order to move forward you need to know that there is nothing I can change about that day. I can work on this day to make it better than the day before. You cant jam pack all your troubles in one day, that's too much for you too bear. Just sit back and relax one day. Sit by yourself and cry, talk about that week, what went wrong, how too fit it and make it better.

Giving up doesn't make you weak, letting go makes you stronger. Holding on to what you know you shouldn't have makes you not only weak but makes you human. Our fears make us hold on to what we have and show a side not worth showing. Giving up on yesterdays problems doesn't mean they aren't going to be there so deal with them and don't hold them off because holding off just builds up anger and frustration.

I left Michigan July 07th 2009. With no piece of mind, no sanity, no sense of stability, no love, compassion, feeling abandoned, confused, scared heartless and cold. I go with hope in my eyes but fear in my heart. I know deep down apart of me wants to go but go back to what? A broken home, where we go days without speaking, where I hold so much anger, hostility, resentment, and disappointment. To a house where it will never be a home because as a family we are divided and broken. I just want to close my eyes to escape from it all. To leave reality and go to dream land because anythings better than here. And I have no worries I have no fears, no thoughts, no regrets, no emotion, and no reasons to turn back.

I am changed, I know I am changed. I have changed for the worst and now I am changed for the best. I am changed because change was intended recommended and suggested not from the lips of anyone else but I. I am changed I have grown changed from all I ever known, what I thought, felt and seen. To live out my goals and live out my dreams. I am changed, I know I am changed. And I didn't do it to please anyone other than myself. I am changed it was what wanted and more so what I needed. Not all change is good, but knowing that why way things are is a step of progression.

I changed my life for the right reasons due to the right people. I changed for a baby named Bri Bri because I never knew how it felt to have someone come into my life and make me want to do better. I wanted to live in the future for her to be someone she could and would look up too. I changed because Bri Bri changed me, emotionally, psychically, mentally, and spiritually, she put my priorities in the right place and changed my frown into a smile.

I changed for a woman named April, and not just any woman. A strong single independent though at times confusing woman. A woman who blessed me with life a woman who though I don't agree with her I am grateful to call her my mother. I changed for a man and not just any may a strong African American man who is my father Carl. I changed because I now understand what he tried to teach me. No man wants a girl, every man wants a woman. I changed that look of resentment and frustration to a look of thankfulness that he stands by me.

Most of all I changed for a man named Jesus. Yes im not perfect and was born in sin I was born of the world, into a world I knew nothing about. I changed because I wanted to live not for myself but for God.

I changed yes I have changed not because you told me too but because I wanted too. Changes are the means to a new beginning, changes are what makes us smiling with satisfaction that we've done something right. But the real thing about change is that you have to know why is it you want to change, think about the lives you are changing for. Think long and hard that is this change going to change your life for the better.

The secret to happiness is finding out who and what makes you happy. Placing everyone where they should be. Getting your feelings out because bottling them in takes a toll on you and wears you down. I don't think pleasing people is a priority of mine any longer. All I worry about is getting through each day a day at a time. I don hold hate or grudges in my heart I learned to pray for not only them but myself that I'll have the strength to forgive them.

I thrive on acceptance, my life depends on what others thought about me. If someone wasn't happy neither was I. The only person I need approval from is God. There will be times when man himself will give up on me but God never will. When I have given up on myself and can't make it on my own. You have to understand that man can not save you, and some days for that matter you can not even save yourself. All you can do is believe.

I believe the reason why so many of my people are stuck in the dark is because the fail to realize that they are living amongst the world and not for it. We don't have faith like we used too. The rate of unsaved people has increased like the number of children in the world over the last couple of years. I know I was one of those people who said I'd get on the straight and narrow after I was done having my fun, which was when I got good and grown with a family of my own. I can't think like that because what happens if I was to die tomorrow? I know for damn sure I'd spend all of forever in hell. So now I at least attempt to live better. I try and clean up my usage of profanity. I don't wear as many shirts with provocative messages anymore.

A lot of us look at it as the world and everyone in it owes us something. I believed it, but the question is what is it I owe the world? I along with just about everybody else have stripped Mother Nature of her innocence, we have raped her and left her out to try. She's not as holy as she used to be. The world was a good girl who's gone bad. I learned that money is not the root of all evil the love and lust for money is. The love for money brings out the worse in all of us who fall victim to it's charm. People do spiteful and low down dirty things because they are lustful. I've lost all that I've worked for in my life because I wanted more. I was being greedy and didn't understand that the best things in life are free. That they are already given and placed right where they should be.

We must understand that the things we value and cherish can be taken away but the one thing that can's is our salvation. We need to believe in the most high and mightiest element there is. If we can do this we can do anything, because God won't let his children be without. And all we have to do is just ask with a clean and open heart and trust in him and only him. If I die anytime soon I would hope that I live on a people remember me for who I was and not someone I wasn't. I believe that the people will feel me on everything I say because I speak for them, I am one of those people. I was blessed with a gift like all of you, I have a talent and I refuse to let it go to waste. Everybody's good at something and if I can tell you only one thing is that I believe in you. Even when your to foolish to believe in yourself know that Ericka will support you and be that voice saying never give up.

I'm not afraid to fall in love, I'm jus afraid to love the wrong person
I'm not afraid to be happy, I'm jus afraid of being sad

I'm not afraid of success, but I know somewhere down the line failures gonna try and get me

I'm not afraid to speak my mind, I'm jus afraid of your reaction

I'm not afraid of the dark, I'm afraid of what lies under the light

I'm not afraid of who you were, I'm more afraid of who your becoming

I'm not afraid to say I LOVE YOU, I'm afraid of the one I love not saying I LOVE You back

I'm not afraid of life, I'm terrified of the life after

I'm not afraid of losing all I own, As long as I still have you

I'm not afraid to reach for the stars

I'm not afraid of me

I'm not afraid to live out loud

I'm not afraid to cry

I'm not afraid to go above and beyond

I'm not afraid to hit the ground, that's jus the risk you take when falling.

It isn't so much about finding yourself as long as you don't lose yourself in the process. I used to laugh at people that told me it took them all their life to find themselves. How is it that you can lose yourself? You of all people should know exactly where you're at? How can you lose what's right in front of you? It wasn't that they lost themselves physically but mentally. The mind goes through more burdens than the body can handle. It took me actually having loss myself to get understand what those people were talking about. I didn't want to be one of those people to always wonder what if? I lost myself years ago, when I moved from New Jersey a small town called Sicklerville. The same town, where I found myself six years and, seven months and five days later. When I found myself it was strange, like I saw some little girl sitting on my old door step cold and afraid, she had been crying and she looked up at me and said where have you been, I've been waiting on you every since you left back in 2002.

The only thing that I could tell her was, *I am so sorry, I couldn't tell you were I was going, because I hadn't known where I been. I'm actually happy I found you, I had no clue where you went running off too*, but it was me who was running all along, I was running away from the one person I was. I was running away from myself.

Where have you been all this time?

In the same place you left me.

I just needed to be home, a place where I felt safe, secure and comfortable. In the state of mind that its never too late. I needed some time to figure out how to make sense of it all. There's no place like home, and there's no place I'd rather be.

Most of the things in my life are broke, but still whole. There is still time to repair the damage that life has caused me, which sadly I brought on myself. Everything happens for a reason, I always wanted to know that reason. And the reason being, bad things happen so we can appreciate the good in life. People hurt you so you learn how to rely on yourself. Friends become foes, they'll put bro's before hoes, people can turn on you in a second and you don't trust everyone in your business, because your closest friends will one day become your closest enemy.

It took a lot of pain, sweat and tears for me to begin to smile and a lot of heart ache to appreciate the little things, because those little things mean so much. In life you make friends and lose friends but it's real friend who are everlasting. No matter the struggles, the fights or distance, real friends are never too far away. Love is expressed in a way that not even the most complicated words can describe. You try and find the words but no word is ever good enough. You can love in the way you look into someone's eyes. How gentle you touch them and how warm you make them feel. How you know whens something's wrong without being told. Life is full of mistakes but no matter if it was in the past you still have time to correct it. Time waits for no one, except the people who use it wisely.

I have written a couple of steps to recovery, to help you get your life back in order.
1. Acknowledgment, change starts with yourself
2. Why are you changing? What is it that your changing and why? Not all change is good
3. List all the things about you that you want to improve
4. Delete all the negativity, such as people on facebook, out of your phone and out of your life completely
5. Love yourself, nobody can love you as well as you can
6. Do what's best for you, nobody else has your best interest
7. Letting go doesn't make you weak, it means your strong enough to walk away
8. Forgiveness, isn't what you do for other people but for yourself
9. Smiling, is contagious and will make a bitch mad
10. Never get mad at the past, theres a reason it didn't make it to your future
11. It's ok to cry, as long as you get it out and let it go
12. Pick and chose your friends wisely, they say a lot about you
13. Those who laugh with you, will secretly laugh at you

14. Being able to laugh at yourself
15. Don't regret the things you've done, only the things you didn't do when you had the opportunity
16. If it doesn't feel right 9 times outta 10 it isn't
17. Remember the most powerful weapon you have is your tongue so chose your words wisely
18. Let your words not only be your actions but your actions be your words
19. People remember us not only by what you say, but what you do
20. Don't stand for everything, you'll fall for anything
21. Ignorance is the ugliest trait and characteristic
22. Make today better than yesterday
23. Your day is influenced by the way you feel
24. Set your standards high and never settle for anything less
25. If you say there isn't a problem, you'll never find a solution
26. Only a fool does the same thing over and over, and expects different results
27. Only when you are no longer afraid is when you begin to live (Dorthy Thomspon)
28. A man who doesn't trust himself can never trust anyone else (Cordinal de Rete)
29. At the end of the day it isn't what they call you, but what you answer to (Tyler Perry ,Madea)

Things We've Learned Lately
Love all, trust a few. Do wrong to none.

The most important thing I've learned is that is isn't always about what you know or how you feel. It's what you learn at the end of the day. It's if you were able to learn the lesson or keep living your life full of mistakes? Alex taught me *that with every breath there's hope.* Now whenever I take a breath I know there's light at the end of any tunnel. There are no regrets just lessons learned, and only a fool makes the same mistake twice. Somebody tell me, how is it that one day can change everything? Why is it that sometimes today was better than yesterday? You went to sleep crying and today you wake up smiling. It seems as if it's not enough hours in the day but a lot can happen in 24 hours. Rain turns into showers, smiles are now frowns, love finds comfort in hate and when you look in the mirror you can't recall your own face?

If you were going to die soon and had only one phone call you could make, who would you call and what would you say? And why are you waiting?

Stephen
Levine

Tell those you love that you love them and how much they mean to you because you never know when your going to get a chance to tell them. Hug them kiss them smile at them and don't hold a grudge. We wait to tell them how we feel because we think we have forever and a lifetime to tell them, but we don't. And I wish that I would have learned that earlier in life because I've waited to long and lost a lot of loved ones that way. Things can change in the blink of an eye and pass up you and you not even notice it. Seeing you smile makes me smile, so when im sad smile at me Smiles are contagious. It takes seventy-two muscles to frown, but only thirteen to smile. You never know what smiling can do for a person.

I've learned that Distance is the hardest thing to overcome. Because distance is just a test to see how far our love can travel.

Nastasha Lowery
When you're in a relationship with someone you truly love being away from them is the hardest thing you ever had to do. Not being able to see their face, feel their touch, hear their voice, and just know that they're never out of arms reach.

I've learned that three little words can set you free. To be able to find happiness and completion I forgive you.

Ericka Newman
I've always been one on forgiving because I know how it feels to have something not be as what I thought. People hurt each other all the time even when they don't know it. The hardest love is the love that you don't even know you had. Forgiving is easier said then done, so remember that you aren't doing that person any harm by not forgiving your only hurting yourself. As I stated before Forgiveness is not what we do for other people, but it is what we do for ourselves to heal, and to move on.

I've learned that love is walking beside someone not behind them or in front.

ShonTorria Edwards

152

When you walk beside someone you walk together in unity as one. Walking behind someone means that they take control and hold the power. Walking in front of them means you don't give a shit about them because you're in charge. It takes a loving heart to walk beside someone showing that you are equal and the same that no one is above or below the other.

I've learned that for some the hardest thing to be is themselves.

Emoni Thornton

It's so easy to be what others want us to be but it's hard as shit to be who we want. I found that it's simpler to please others than to please yourself. People don't have the high expectations that you have for yourself. They don't care if you make it or fail. Being who you are is when you don't care what others think but keep others best interest as well as yours at hand. Change is only for the best when your changing for yourself.

I've learned that you don't have to search for love because it's been right there in your face.

Erica Hammerbacher

You search high and low for something that's been in your vision you were just over looking it. I found the greatest love of all is the love that you don't have to look all over the place for. Love that will be waiting for you till the end of time and will never leave you because things aren't going as planned. People don't understand that all you have to do is have an open heart to the unacceptable and unexplainable.

The one thing that I've truly learned is that there is something's that I'll just never understand and I'm okay with that. Maybe I'm not ready or just don't need to know. What if things fall into place for a reason? Like with Haiti how can we repair someone else's homeland when we haven't even finished helping the victims of Hurricane Katrina? I'll never understand why people are homeless and why we are facing a recession? I'll never understand why parents get divorced or why some of us are taken up to Heaven. I'll never be able to understand why we pay attention to those who pay us no mind, and pay no mind to those who pay us attention? Why we say I love to the ones who don't love us? I'll never be able to why people cheat, why they lie and hurt those they claim to love? I'll never understand hate, jealousy and envy and why it takes control of girls turning the sweetest ones into cold hearted bitches. I'll never understand if hearts aren't meant to be broken why do we break them?

Like Dr. Martin Luther King Jr, I have a dream, that one day our nation will live up to their word, when they said that all men were created equal. The equality that our four fathers spoke of was a lie that equality never existed. The equality we dreamed of was only temporary, to satisfy and shut the black man up, thinking it would end segregation. We will never love let alone respect thy neighbor, there will always be something standing in the way. Man has been looked down upon for being too light, too tall, too short, or too dark, for not being smart enough or thinking they know it all. Man has been looked down upon for the color of his skin, but never for his thoughts or the contents of his character. You can take every material possession he owns, but not his thoughts for those are one of the few things that belong to him. You cannot hate a man, for what he believes in, what he values in life is what he will die for. If there isn't something worth dying for, there is nothing to live for.

I have a dream, that we will one day be able to see each other in the same light. To see past one another's imperfections and see everyone with the same that no one man is set higher than any other. That we can all hold hands as brothers and sisters and not let our fears get in the way. I wish that interracial love was the same as any other love. I believe love sees no color, there is no white or black only shades of gray. You can't fault love for who it falls in love with.

I have a dream that we will learn to fight with our words and not our fists. That when faced with even the most difficult times we could talk out our problems and solve our differences without violence, but with an open mind, and an open heart. Malcolm X said by any means necessary but what means are truly necessary? Violence and hatred are simply the causes of ignorance. Actions speak louder than words, so let your words be your actions, and your actions be your words.

Against Thee Odds
I crawled, I climbed, I walked and ran
To find something within my inner man
I was beaten, battered and yes I was bruised
I never gave up because I refused to lose
I fell time and time and time again
My determination I was destined to win
I was lost with no direction, misguided and confused
People had degraded me leaving me helpless, sorry and used
When they told me I couldn't do it
I was out to seek them wrong
Not only am I brave, most of all I am strong
I told myself I'd reach the mountain top
I couldn't quit and wouldn't stop
I didn't care how long it would take
I kept striving without any break
At times it was hard
But the hardship was worth it
Don't let anyone get in the way of your dreams
And say you don't deserve it

There's times when you give up, give in and times when you just stop caring. Well I finally stopped caring, I came to a crossroad and didn't know where I was supposed to be. I stopped caring about what made everyone else happy and focused on my own happiness. There were people that didn't believe in me and still don't. I've been told *"You ain't shit and ain't never gonna be shit"* I knew right then that I had to prove them wrong. In my eyes there is no such thing as a lost cause. I feel as if a lot of us are just lacking guidance and understanding. I feel as if I'm living proof that if I can do it so can anybody. I look at my life as a big ass pile of confusion only because I needed to get to this point so I could reach out to others. I finally stopped being what everybody wanted me to be and started being who I needed to be. I'm gonna be all that you said I couldn't all that you said I wasn't able or capable of being. Im gonna be more than anyone expected. Not to prove you wrong but prove myself that I can be anything I set myself to be.

No Privacy

Sometimes having your life out in the open and your privacy invaded can be a good thing. I let my guard down and now I am finally able to move on and start my new life. My life consists of no secrets, no lies, no regrets or grudges all I have is a new aspect and lessons learned. In this lifetime its okay to cry, to have flaws and to get heartbroken. Nobody truly understands that you can't make it through life as if nothing bothers you. It's okay to admit your not perfect and that things wont always go your way, it's okay that you don't know where your going but you need to come to a point when you say who I am isn't who I used to be. I'm learning that people change & you'll make mistakes, but life goes on. I'm old enough to know the difference between right and wrong. Sadly not everybody is like me and not everybody can make basic decisions for themselves.

There are three types of people in this world. People who make things happen, people who watch things happen, and people who say what happened? People who live in the world and people who live of the world. We think that the world owes us because we are here. Nobody asked to be here and nobody truly asks to leave. I think that life is a cycle that repeats it's self and gets worse each time around. I look at my generation as the lost generation. People say that things have changed and we have no respect, but I say look at who it is that raised us.

To achieve your dreams remember your ABC'S

A- avoid negative people, places, things and old habits
B- believe in yourself
C- consider things from every side
D- don't give up, don't give in
E- enjoy life today, yesterday is gone and tomorrow isn't promised.
F- Forgives is the best revenge
G- Go after your dreams
H- Hang on to your dreams
I- Ignore ignorance
J- Just do it
K- Keep trying no matter how hard it seems
L- Love yourself then love others
M- Make room for improvement
N- Never bring people down
O- Open your mind as well as your heart
P- Practice makes perfect
Q- Quitters never win
R- Respect yourself as well as others

S- Stand up for what you believe in
T- Take control of your life
U- Understand that life isn't always fair
V- Violence is never the answer
W- Winners never quit
X- Xpect more
Y- You are one of a kind
Z- Zero tolerance for nothing less than your best

People ask me all the time what was I trying to achieve when I wrote this. The only thing I was trying to do was write a piece of literature that would inspire a nation. To let people know there's more than what meets the eye. I wanted to show sides of me that nobody knew that I didn't even know was there. I wanted to paint a vivid, clear image of who Ericka was, is and wants to be. I want talents to be recognized and discovered, like myself people underestimated me and some knew I always had it in me. I just needed to prove it to myself that my life wasn't a lost cause. I wanted to define who I was and speak out for my sisters, all my sisters. We are more alike in many ways. I don't care how many times you say that this would never be you but there's a little me in all of us.

I wanted to give a girl with a broken heart and broken sprit her confidence and self-esteem back. One of the biggest reasons why so many people fail is because they don't believe in themselves. When you raise your voice it becomes louder than the crowd. Any fight is a good fight as long as it's worth fighting for and no I don't mean a boy. I wanted to let the girl reading this book know that she is beautiful inside and out. That even though every girl wants to be complimented not everyone is going to want to compliment you that sometimes you have to compliment yourself. Love yourself because if you don't know one else will.

I wanted to remind us to get intact with ourselves, about who we are and what we want. I wanted to ask how bad is you're want too, you're want to change to be and do better? To tell everyone that what we want may not be the same as everyone else. Two people can here the same message and interpret it in two different ways. You may want love and happiness and someone else may want lust and satisfaction. Different people want different things and will go different lengths to get what they want.

One thing that will keep you from success is our pride, it will keep you caged and make you ignorant. You may need help but you reject it because you have too much pride. And it's okay to ask for help, I wish I had asked for help. A lot of the things I went through could have been avoided if I had asked or taken someone's advice but I didn't want to look weak and admit I was wrong. Your pride will eat you up inside and make you a heartless person who thinks they can go through life alone.

I wanted to bring a family closer, I wanted to tell what goes on in most teenage girls mindsets. I wanted to expose how feelings can get the best of us and how easy it is to be victimized of love and promises. I wanted to give leadership to myself and those who think like me. I want to build communication and build trust. I wanted barriers to be broken and voices to be heard.

Life is about the journey not the destination, and the longest journey begins with a single step. Life is what you make it, if you want something go by force and take it. Don't let anyone tell you that you aren't good enough, because it doesn't matter what they say about you but what you say about yourself. Who cares what they think, all that matters is what you think of yourself.

I sat down and cried today at the thought my life will never be the same, my house will never be a home and the fact that my parents are both single parents. I cried because the family I knew that was tight like glue fell apart and there was nothing I could do. I cried today for my sister, I cried for my mom, I cried for my dad and most of all I cried for myself. I cried because people hurt me and continue to hurt me, only because I let them.

I sat down and cried today, because over the years I burned a lot of bridges, some are better off burned and some you always wonder? I cried because again the things in my life are broken, and will never be the same. Friends gone away with the wind, it's like I stand in front of total strangers hoping things could go to the way they were before. I cried because instead of letting go, I held on so tightly, and made things even worse. I bit the hand that fed me, I made this monster, and now I have to deal with it, but I don't have to live in it. I cried because for the first time I actually started doing what was right for Ericka.

I sat down and cried today, not because I was sad, but for the first time I cried because I was happy. I cried today not because I was feeling weak, but I cried because I was strong enough to overcome it. I cried because things are now starting to make sense, I cried over the friends I've lost, but I cried as well as of those I've gained who are close to my heart. I cried because I found love. The kinda love you can only imagine or read in a fairytale. I sat on the bed and thanked God for this day, the day that I was able to wake up, not just get up but GROW UP. I cried because I learned that in order to forgive others, I must forgive myself. I know my future will be nothing like my past. I'm moving forward and am never going back.

Hell I cried because letting it out every once in a while helps me cope. I cried because I finally faced it, and though I didn't want too I did it. I over came my fear of acceptance. I don't care what people think because this is my life and I have too live it, no one can live it for me. I cried because I wanted too, I cried because I needed too and most of all I cried because I knew it needed to be done.

Forgiveness

I hate you, I hate you, I hate you
For giving me this feeling, this hell of a feeling. A feeling I can't even begin to explain, not even words could describe. A feeling I never knew I was capable of feeling
I hate you, I hate you, I hate you,
For putting this twinkle in my eye. I'd scribble your name in my notebook with little hearts your name and mine, you and me forever. Your picture in my locker, on my binder and in my room, you gave me butterflies and I liked it
I hate you, I hate you, I hate you
For remembering the little things, because those little things made a big difference. Like remembering my favorite color, my favorite book, favorite food, candy and day of the week, for remembering what makes me smile as well as mad. For remembering the first time we met, hung out, the first time we kissed. You kept every picture, every letter
I hate you, I hate you, I hate you,
For saying I love you, for making me believe that it was true, that I was special, and what we had was real. This was what I had been waiting for, longed for, hoped for and could only dream about.
I hate you, I hate you, I hate you
Because one day you didn't feel like trying anymore. You were ready to give up and I wasn't ready to give in. I was taught every fight was a good fight as long as it was worth fighting for. I held on so tightly you slipped right out of my hands.
I hate you, I hate you, I hate you
For giving me this feeling, this got damn feeling that now that I have it I can't get rid of it, I can't let it go. My smile is gone and is never

coming back, and it's all because of you and your selfishness. Why can't I shake you, why can't I just be free.

I hate you, I hate you, I hate you

That twinkle in my eye are now tears, that won't stop dripping from my face. I scribble your name out of my notebook. Take down all the photos of you I have those butterflies are gone you make me sick to my stomach. You're like scum between my toes.

I hate you, I hate you, I hate you

For everything you remembered because now its everything I cant forget. You tease me with my letters, throw them back in my face to embarrass me, to hurt me, to tease me, to taunt me and haunt me, and remind me of the past.

I hate you, I hate you, I hate you

For telling me you loved me, now why would you do such a thing if you know damn well you didn't mean it? I gave you a piece of me, a piece of me you didn't ask for, a piece of me you didn't earn, let alone deserve.

I hate you, I hate you, I hate you

Because you're the only face I see, the only voice I hear. The only one I want and the fact you don't feel the same makes me hate you more.

I hate you, I hate you, I hate you

My most important lesson I was trying to teach was Forgiveness. Forgiveness is accepting what was, what is, dealing with it, not forgetting it and having the will power to bigger and better yourself. Everybody needs to be forgiven, even if you don't want to or think they deserve it. Forgive those who hurt you, because being and staying mad isn't bothering them. Consuming hate in your heart will only bother you, and you're the only one left feeling bitter at the end of the day.

I forgave a lot of people for a lot of things but before I could forgive any of them I had to first forgive myself. I was mad at those especially those who had so called love for me. People hurt people all the time, I look at it this way, everyone's human and they do things we don't approve of but that doesn't stop them from doing it. Forgiveness is giving up my right to hurt you because you hurt me. Forgiveness is not granted because a person deserves it but out of acts of mercy and love. By forgiving others we free ourselves.

Ephesians 4:31-32

Get rid of all bitterness, rage, anger, harsh words and slander as well as all types of malicious behavior. Instead be kind to each other, forgiving just as God through Christ has forgiven you.

No Privacy

Mother, I don't know what I'd do without mine. She gave me life and would remind me just as she gave me life she could take it away whenever I disobeyed and disrespected her. Though my mother seemed unreasonable at times, hell all the time she was still my mother and I was proud to call her that. I respected her only for the fact that she tried. She stood in my corner when nobody else would, but wasn't that her responsibility as my mother? I felt she obligated to love me and take care of me more so to love me when I acted like a total jackass.

If I could tell my mommy anything, it would be thank you because I'm glad that she cared. I saw children whose parents who did not care what they did. My mom refused to let me run the streets like some hoodlum. Although the love was there it should have been in another form. I wanted my mom to talk to me. So we can see eye to eye on what was going on. A conversation means much more than any punishment. The hardest thing to do is to explain to those you love how you really feel without raising your voice or hurting their feelings. If I could tell my mommy anything it would be that I love her because I feel as if that's the one thing that I lack to tell her, without her there is no me.

If I could tell my dad anything, I would reassure him that a little faith goes a long way. We have made it this fair by faith and not by sight. There were times when I said fuck it, but my dad never gave up and never gave in. This was when I realized that at this given moment there was only one male figure besides Christ in my life and he was it. He was the only male that ever truly gave me the love and attention that not only I wanted, and needed but deserved. He could be a prick at times, and I felt he was stubborn and too old to change his ways, but as rough as my dad appeared on the surface, he was a big ass baby just like me. My dad, not to say he was a push over, but there was a lot more things that I got away with, with him then I ever could with my mom.

I felt that my dad sheltered me too much, he was living in the past treating me like the little 9 year old I was when I last saw him, but she was long gone. Then there were times he treated me too much like an adult, I'm down for responsibility and all but got damn, paying you gas money. I look in the mirror, and I see that spitting image everyone talks about, I try and deny it but its there. I get a lot of my logical thinking from my peanut head ass father, and not the fuck the world and everyone in it logic.

Louie,

I think I have the most ill feelings towards you because you and I both know you used me. One thing we can agree on is that, our night was nothing more than pure lust! You were young and I was even younger. Till this day, I always wondered why me? Was it because I was the new girl? Was it you wanted someone who wasn't like those other bitches at school? You took something from me that I can never get back. Actually you took a lot more; you took my virginity, my innocence, my sanity, my privacy, space and ability to use good judgment. I see you, and can't forget you. Want to speak but I choke, because I have no idea what to say too you. I told myself when I ever saw you again I would slap the hell out of you, and there are times I just want too talk to you, to catch up and other days it's better off that never ever speak a word, think a thought about you or even look your way. You will always be apart of me though the thought of it makes me sick, makes me cry at night, the thought of the first boy I ever had sex with was a jerk makes me truly dislike boys in general. But I forgive you, I forgive what happened because it's nothing I can do about it.

Dear Quason,

The way things played out only made us dislike each other, when all I ever wanted was for us to keep in touch. Deep down beneath all that tough boy hood shit, your super duper sweet, and im sad I got to realize that when I was miles and miles away. I feel as if we never really gotten the chance to know one another, or to ever spend time together. They say time heals all but no not really, all time does is create a false hope. All time does it keeps the tears from falling but when they do fall the flow like waterfalls constantly, because you thought there was something. All time does is make the situation worse especially when you don't know what to do in the first place. I'm so at a loss for words because one minute it's good and the next we done hit rock bottom. And I'm tired of not knowing what's in store for the next day. I cared for you when you were down and out. Stood by you even when I didn't have too, but the real question isn't if I care for you but do you care for me? Even if I ask you I still will second guess if you're telling me the truth or what I just want to hear. And I just want to know was it real or just a front. I think it was too soon for us to be using the "L" word because for as long as we claim to have loved one another I wasn't even in the state. But its time to cut the bullshit and be real, I deserve that much from you. I'm tired of the games, the false hope and the lies. We'll never be anything more than what we are now, and that's the reality of it. But what are we? Are we two people just living our lives doing our own thing and when we see each other we put on a front and act like all head over 'heals like we really were missing each other? Where do we go from here? At one point in time we weren't even speaking and then when we did speak I felt like I was doing all the talking, or we were just listening to each other breath and I don't want that, and the moment I say ok we need to just stay friends you come out of the blue and we just laugh and talk and I get that reassurance I had been wanting and I get right back confused. I guess what I'm trying to say is that I want to end this on a good note but goodbyes are never ended the way you want, I wish you the best of luck in all you do.

Dear Tarun

No matter the hurt and confusion I feel, I still got so much love for you. All I can say was maybe if I lived there we could have a chance. I wish you would have been more honest but then again I can't blame you because honestly we was both on that bullshit. Though we were honest we were only honest to a certain extent. I still have the biggest crush on you, I try and look past what you do but it's your actions that speak louder than any words you try to say to comfort me. I don't hate you, personally, I just hate who you've become. You've become a distant friend, pretty much a stranger and I want to remember you as the same Tarun I met in August, the same Tarun I talked too every night about any and everything. I still think your sweet, though I feel we've become distant towards one another and it shouldn't be that way. Our friendship shouldn't have to suffer. What was fighting Kooda going to solve? Nothing, all it would do was make it seem like we were fighting over you and I told you I refused to let that happen. And when I saw the picture of you and her on facebook I wanted to say something about it, but I see you took it down. When you kissed me I kept my eyes open, because I never wanted to lose the sight of you. When you kissed me I smiled, because this was the moment that I felt so alive. And when I left I closed my eyes so I could see your face, and the moment I felt so alive a little bit of me died on the inside.. It's as if you owe me, what do you owe me? Besides my money, you owe me the got damn truth, aren't I worth that much? Is our friendship, relationship based on a lie? You lied, you lied to me, lied to me about not feeling the need to ever lie to me. "I wish I could believe you and I'd be alright, and now everything you told me really don't apply to the way I feel inside, loving you was easy once upon a time, but now my suspicions of you, they multiply and it's all because you lied."- Beyonce. The thing that hurts the most about being lied to is knowing you aren't worth the truth. I understand that your going through a lot, but your not the only one, and yet with all I'm going through I can still pick up the phone to call you, to check on you, and be the friend that you aren't being to me. I hate that it seems like your avoiding me, and whatever the case may be, I wish you well, I want you to live up to your full potential because I got to see past all that hood shit into the real you or so I thought. I forgive you Tarun, and even if we never speak another word I hope life treats you well.

Dear Edrick,
    I finally forgive you…..
    I finally know what it means to forgive someone. It means letting go of all those unsettled feelings, being able to accept what was as nothing more than what it used to be, not forgetting the past but moving toward the future. Being able to stop regretting what happened and not letting it affect you anymore. Before I never thought I could ever find it in my heart to forgive you but I grew up and realized in life people are gonna hurt you, but it means nothing to seek revenge. All this time I thought I was doing the right thing but doesn't make it the right thing. I thought I was helping but I was only making matters worse. By refusing to let go it only made us grow apart, it hurt me and made me hate you more. And I don't wanna hate you or anybody else for that matter. I told you I was a lover not a fighter, but I fight for what I love, but honestly what was I fighting for? I held on to someone who wanted too leave a long time ago, but never wanted to admit it. Every time you were in a new relationship you were gone with the wind and weren't heard from until that relationship was over. I fully accept that there will never be ANYTHING between us, ever again and are better off not speaking. We said our friendship was strong enough to last a lifetime and could overcome anything. But you couldn't balance our friendship and your girlfriends hatred towards the fact that you were friends and good friends with a female you broke up with. E-roc, I don't want you back especially after what I know now, but what happened to Edrick, my Edrick, not only my friend but, my best friend Edrick? Who knew me better than anybody Edrick? I forgive you but don't think for one second I did it for you because I'm doing it for myself. I heard that one day my wounds will heal, but deep down those old wounds never fully fucking heal or back to its original state. They just get covered up, all I thought I ever needed was closure, but you can never really get closure there's no way to become satisfied when the one you thought you loved breaks your heart over and over again. "I'd catch a grenade for ya, throw my hand on a blade for ya, jump in front of a train for ya, you know I'd do anything for ya, go through all this pain, take a bullet straight to the brain, yes I

164

would die for you baby, but you wont do the same."- Bruno Mars. People come into our lives for a reason, make you smile to make up for when your sad, tell a joke to lighten the mood, Even if it's just for a second, a minute, or a week. And you Edrick, you have impacted and been a big influence and guide in my life for the last four years. And not for one second would I take it back. I didn't write this too go and relive the past, but in order to move on I must confront it, something I never wanted to do. But in life we don't do what we want to do but what we have to and must do.

E-rock
It wasn't a breakdown but a breakthrough

E-rock was everything I wasn't, everything I didn't stand for, nothing like I thought she should be, then again I had no expectation of her. Her qualities were my insecurities everything I was lacking was what made E-rock who she was. I loved that she was so outspoken and never bit her tongue, some people feared her some couldn't stand her but she was respected. Some words are better left unsaid and some words there are just no words to fix the words you said in the first place. She was a bitch, but deep down every bitch has a soft spot. Her love is so strong it became vicious but she means well. She was protective of those she loved and would do anything for them

She puts up this wall and most people know how to get over it or tear it down, because deep down she's as sweet as pie. I look at her now, weak, helpless she was so quick to fight and now it seems as if she's paralyzed. She can't even ball up her fist, there's nothing that she can do to hurt me now. I reach out my hand to try and save her but she knows as well as I do it was her time to go. She's at peace now no longer is she trying to be tough to not let anyone in her life because she feels she can't be broken. I look at her thinking that poor girl used to be me. I used to be that girl with to much pride who acted as if it was a sin to ask for help, I was that girl stuck in the dark afraid to turn on the light because I didn't know what I was going to see.

I was the one person who truly and ever gave a damn about E-rock and she was constantly treating me like shit hurting those she loved but that's all she knew, she didn't know what it meant to love someone who loves you for everything your not, to never judge you but stand by you. I was her biggest critic I knew what was best for her, what was best for me. "Nobody knows that deep down I tried to make people like me because that's all I ever wanted was for people to like me and for someone to love me and I never got that. I became so bitter so defensive and hurt a lot of people and I hope they forgive me. I was fighting myself in a fight that either way I was going to lose. Because I was hurting myself and now there's no fixing the damaged I've caused."

I think that everything happens for a reason and everybody started out as nothing and it's their choice if they stay nothing or become somebody. I have the most respect for her that she stood up for what she believed in but then it came to a point when she stood up for anything, she had no values no reason there wasn't anything that she really wouldn't defend. Though I lost myself at times, at the end of the day it made me love myself more.

It's hard knowing, the one person that you hate is yourself. It's hard knowing that it's your fault why your life went wrong. You want to blame somebody else so you can feel better but you can't. You look back at the past and cry, you get mad at yourself because you knew better but you still did the things you did anyway. You have common sense and good judgment but didn't use it.

I knew better with a lot of the things I did, and I can't help but wonder why did I do it? Because I'm human and we all make mistakes, but the thing about mistakes is that you can learn from them and if you decide to do it again it's because you wanted too. Every battle I have ever fought was because I always felt I had something to prove to someone. But the only person I needed to ever prove something too was to me. But sadly back then what I thought didn't matter, everybody else's opinion mattered. I wanted people to think of me in a good way and that only made them think badly. I gave people the opportunity and the right to tell me who I was and who I should be. But who knows me better than me? Who knows what's right and what's wrong in my life?

The moment you give your rights and thoughts to other people you life is no longer yours. People will tell you that you're ugly but you're only ugly if you believe it. You're only a failure when you give up and stop trying.

The last thing E-rock told me was that she didn't want to leave feeling purposeless. And at that moment I knew she accomplished her goal, she told her story through me. She told me that she isn't afraid of death she's afraid of dying without a sense of completion. "My one wish isn't to be everything to everybody but to be something to someone." It's a tough pill to swallow when you have no one in your corner because you hurt them and pushed them away. I always wanted respect but I never gave it. I saw that people were afraid of my craziness and I was afraid of myself, I didn't know who E-rock was anymore, and I knew that it was time to let go.

I looked in the mirror and for the first time I liked what I was seeing, I was seeing the real me, for the first time in a long time I was proud of who I was I liked who I was, I'm finally comfortable with who I am. And at that very moment when I accepted who I was and I forgave her because I forgave myself.

I am Ericka, I will always be Ericka. I like everything about Ericka because Ericka is me. Ericka is strong though at times she's weak, at times she cries but Ericka is human but there is nothing that Ericka can't overcome.

Made in the USA
Monee, IL
18 June 2021